HUNTINGDONSHIRE
IN THE SECOND WORLD WAR

HUNTINGDONSHIRE
IN THE SECOND WORLD WAR

CAROLINE CLIFFORD AND ALAN AKEROYD
FOREWORD BY **THE RT HON. SIR JOHN MAJOR KG CH**

TEMPUS

First published 2007

Tempus Publishing
Cirencester Road, Chalford
Stroud, Gloucestershire, GL6 8PE
www.tempus-publishing.com

Tempus Publishing is an imprint of NPI Media Group

British Library Cataloguing in Publication Data.
A catalogue record for this book is available from the British Library.

ISBN 978 0 7524 4420 8

Typesetting and origination by NPI Media Group
Printed and bound in Great Britain

Contents

Foreword

There have been two wars in the last century that changed the world. Often, the histories of war are written at a lofty level and concern the ambitions of governments and the strategies of generals.

But the impact of war falls on individuals unconnected with its declaration or its management. These individuals are, most obviously, the soldiers, sailors and airmen, but the largest group upon whom the shadow of war falls are those within communities. The Home Front is part of the war effort too.

How did they cope? What did war mean to them? How did their day-to-day life change? What was the impact on the community? What was life like in Huntingdonshire?

This story is history in its most basic form and in many ways, the most important. If we knew more about life at the grassroots throughout our long history, would not our history be more complete?

In *Huntingdonshire in the Second World War*, Alan Akeroyd and Caroline Clifford have set out the story of war for one community – from the early planning in 1936, to the unsurprising outbreak in 1939 and the long six years that followed with its roller coaster of emotions. The record of our famous Pathfinder Squadron is part of our history – but, for this book, not the main part.

Huntingdonshire in the Second World War will bring back many memories for those who lived through it all. For those who did not, it will explain the sacrifices made by their parents and grandparents to safeguard the freedoms we so take for granted in our own generation.

It is a story worth telling and worth reading – a tribute to the past and a lesson for the future.

Rt Hon. Sir John Major KG CH
August 2007

Introduction and Acknowledgements

We decided to write this book because we were aware that there was no published history devoted to Huntingdonshire during the war years. Although we discovered many fascinating details in the course of our research, we realise that this book is not the definitive account of the Second World War in Huntingdonshire. Nevertheless, we hope that it will offer a vivid insight into this important and dramatic period.

The publication of this book would not have been possible without the assistance of many individuals. We would like to thank Christine May, Head of Archives and Local Studies, for allowing us to reproduce images from the County Record Office in Huntingdon; Chris Jakes of the Cambridgeshire Collection for use of the images from Cambridgeshire Libraries; Andy Veale, editor of the *Hunts Post*, for images from the *Hunts Post* and Bob Burn Murdoch for images from the Norris Museum. Thanks also to Mike Stephenson, Jean Matthews, Nita Luxford and David Cozens for the use of their images. Thanks to Diana Boston, for permission to quote extracts from *Memories* by Lucy Boston; Deana Hudson, for extracts from *Village Memories 1900–2000* by the Upwood and Raveley Local History Group; Margaret Faulkner, for extracts from *A Village Childhood: Great Stukeley 1940–1950*; Richard Hillier of Peterborough Central Library and author of *Clay That Burns*; Crecy Publishing (www.crecy. co.uk) for permission to quote from *Pathfinder* by Air Vice-Marshal Don Bennett and I.B. Hunter for extracts from *Huntingdonshire Revisited 1940–1998*. Thanks also to Pat Whitney, Alexa Cox, the Imperial War Museum, Duxford, and Sue Martin of the FSB Scanning Bureau, and we would especially like to thank the Rt Hon. Sir John Major KG CH, former MP for Huntingdonshire, for writing the foreword.

We have made every effort to track down the copyright owners of all the photos we have used. Any errors that may have occurred are inadvertent and the authors welcome notification of corrections.

Finally, thank you to Lesley and Nick for the patience and encouragement they have shown during the writing of this book.

Alan Akeroyd
Caroline Clifford

CHAPTER I

'Nothing more than Peace, Security, Freedom and Justice': The Outbreak of War

PREPARATIONS FOR WAR

The declaration of war in September 1939 came as no surprise to the people of Huntingdonshire. In 1936 Commander A.S.G. Bell, based in Gazeley House in Huntingdon, had set up preliminary Air Raid Precaution Committees in each of the county's districts, investigating views on the necessary uniforms and equipment and the availability of gas-proof rooms, protective clothing, and respirators. The Home Office had been circulating information about the availability of training in identifying differences between high explosive and incendiary bombs, how to fit respirators, basic first aid, and how to clear up debris following bombing raids.

By August 1936 the County Hospital in Huntingdon was assessing the number of beds it would need in the event of air attack; and in the following month the county's main ARP Committee started to draw up plans for ensuring the robustness of the emergency telephone network. Formal cooperation between Hunts Constabulary and the county's ARP Committee, about how they would respond in the event of German bombing, began in January 1937.

In Huntingdonshire, two air-raid wardens were assigned for every 250 people. In the words of the Regional ARP Controller:

> The Air-Raid Warden will generally be a man, but may be a woman, and will, if possible, live in his own area: he will be a well-known, reliable person of standing and influence among his neighbours, who can be trusted to set an example of coolness and steadiness in an emergency: he will make it his business to get to know not only all the people in his area, but also all the houses and other buildings, all the streets and lanes, gardens and yards, front doors and back doors, besides the position of all water, gas, electric mains, telephones and sewers.

Preparations for war continued apace throughout 1939. In January air-raid wardens in Brampton and Spaldwick had been busy boxing up gas masks ready for

John Rivett-Carnac, Huntingdonshire's Chief Constable and Regional ARP Controller at the beginning of the Second World War. During the First World War Rivett-Carnac had fought in Mesopotamia and India. After D-Day he served as Lieutenant-Colonel in the Military Government of France, Italy and Germany. (County Record Office Huntingdon: 4440/208/80)

immediate distribution to residents and by July gas masks had been delivered everywhere in Huntingdonshire except the villages of Earith and Hemingford Abbots. The early delivery of gas masks proved handy for Somersham resident Mr Macdonald Ruff, who used his to enter a burning smoke-filled house and tackle the blaze.

A National Service Committee and a county branch of the Women's Voluntary Services for Civil Defence (WVS) were formed – chaired by the Earl and Countess of Sandwich respectively. By June there were eighty committees of the WVS at work across the county, preparing depots to supply clothing and other comforts for refugees; 2,842 mattress covers had already been made.

In April the Territorial Field Army had its numbers raised from the peacetime establishment of 130,000 men to a wartime establishment of 340,000, with a further 100,000 in the anti-aircraft section – all to be equipped to the same standards as the regular army. Recruiting evenings were held across the county. A permanent staff instructor, Sgt Freeman, was based in the Drill Hall in St Neots Market Square to advise on joining the regular army and the reserves. In June members of the Territorial Army (TA) were sent on training camps, which raised local fears about not having enough men to bring in the harvest. About 300 officers and men of the 36th Middlesex Anti-Aircraft Battalion of the TA arrived to camp on St Neots Common.

The Empire Air Day festivities at RAF Wyton on 20 May were designed to inform people about the forthcoming war. The programme featured a

Instructions for putting on a service respirator, from *The Advanced Auxiliary Fireman* of 1942. (Cambridgeshire Libraries)

demonstration of shelters and trenches by the ARP. As a thrilling climax to the afternoon, six Blenheim bombers dived down to attack a dummy factory, built of wood. ARP squads then hurried onto the scene to deal with the conflagration and 'casualties'. Ten thousand people visited the show. The government film *The Warning*, giving an 'awesome picture of air war', circulated local cinemas. The Mayor of Huntingdon, W.E. Driver, warned the audience that whether they liked it or not, war could be brought to their doorstep and stressed the need for improving the civil defences. The Borough of Huntingdon was almost up to strength, but there were vacancies elsewhere, particularly at RAF Wyton and Upwood, where personnel for the Operations Room, cooks, butchers, photographers and heavy motor-vehicle drivers were all required.

The threat of air attack meant that towns and villages across Huntingdonshire would have to be blacked out. A practice exercise was planned for the night of 13–14 July, to include fifteen counties across East Anglia. ARP wardens patrolled their sectors to ensure all lights were screened or dimmed. The county control centre, with twelve telephonists and plotting clerks, was set up at the back of Gazeley House in Huntingdon. The report centre in St Ives was at Coote & Warren's garage in Station Road, with ARP posts at Needingworth Road (J.W. Bryant's house), Messrs Judes' garage in the Quadrant; North Road (A. Golding's house), Purser's garage in Green End; and London Road (Mr Eaton's house). The first-aid point was at Dr W.R. Groves' surgery. In Ramsey, an ambulance was stationed at Sycamore's garage. The main first-aid post in

Requisitioned vehicles at Duxford's Imperial War Museum. (The authors)

Huntingdon was the George Street Hall, but there were also twenty-two men and women ambulance drivers and fourteen first-aiders waiting at Murkett's garage. Boy scouts acted as messengers. In all, over 200 people took part in the exercise in Huntingdon, with another fifty-nine at Godmanchester and around fifty at St Neots. RAF planes flew over the area to check the effectiveness of the blackout. They reported that the blackout was almost perfect, although one garage in Ramsey and one in Stilton refused to dim their lights. Several vehicles on the A1 also had full lights or fog lights on. According to the *Hunts Post*:

> The report centre... hummed with activity, and although it was all make-believe, as one stood by and heard reports of death and destruction coming in from all quarters, one could not help visualising the terribly grim scene which would be enacted if ever things reach reality.

One of the biggest challenges proved to be driving through the darkened streets on sidelights, but the *Hunts Post* was pleased to report that even the women drivers came through without a scratch! At the end of August, kerbstones at junctions and bridges were painted with intermittent white lines to help motorists during the blackout.

The exercise in Godmanchester was not so successful, as it relied on nearby Huntingdon for essential services. Once the bridge had been 'blown up', the ambulance had to make a detour via St Ives or St Neots in order to cross the

AIR RAID PRECAUTIONS

HANDBOOK No. 1

(2nd Edition)

PERSONAL PROTECTION
AGAINST GAS

LONDON
HIS MAJESTY'S STATIONERY OFFICE
Price *6d.* net

Government instructions on protection against gas attacks. (Cambridgeshire Libraries)

river. The organisers in St Ives were commended for their initiative in sending the messenger via the railway bridge when the road bridge was 'blown up' and the telephone communications 'cut'. Blackout exercises also took part in other towns and villages such as Offord, Kimbolton and Great Staughton.

A second practice operation was planned for the night of 9–10 August. This was to involve fire, rescue and decontamination squads, with fires at Huntingdon, Fletton, Yaxley, Ramsey, St Ives, St Neots, Godmanchester and Kimbolton; gas attacks at Huntingdon, Yaxley, Ramsey, St Ives and St Neots; and 'other incidents' at Offord, Warboys and Abbots Ripton. Sirens were also to be sounded for the first time. From the outset this exercise did not run smoothly, partly because many of the wardens were on holiday. At 6.00 p.m. on 9 August it was announced that the exercise was being postponed for twenty-four hours. However, it went ahead as planned at Huntingdon, Godmanchester, Ramsey and St Neots, albeit amid great confusion as some people had heard about the cancellation. The exercise in St Ives took place twenty-four hours later.

A few weeks later Germany invaded Poland, and all practices came to an end as war itself became certain. Huntingdonshire was well prepared. The Government had issued booklets and instructions about almost everything – even the fact that pets should be prevented from entering public shelters. Emergency instructions stated that it was unlikely any town in Huntingdonshire would be considered a military target, and that any bombs dropped would probably be those from enemy aircraft 'lightening their load.' Given the speed of German bombers, any

Preparing to Escape from an Upstairs Window.   **Dropping from an Upstairs Window.**

'How to escape from an upstairs window'. From *Air Raids: What you must know, what you must do*, published by the Ministry of Home Security, 1940. (Cambridgeshire Libraries)

town would only be in range for 15 seconds, so a maximum of six bombs would be dropped. Nevertheless, householders were instructed to keep two buckets of earth or sand, two buckets of water and a shovel with a broom handle attached handy to deal with incendiary devices.

The blackout came into force, and by Saturday 2 September it was impossible to buy a yard of dark material in Huntingdon. Black and dark blue cloth of any sort had been sold 'by the mile'. Thick brown paper was then snapped up at 2*d* a sheet. Drawing pins, needed to fix the paper in position, were also at a premium. Evening bus services were curtailed and where they did run, buses would run with their lights out. The conductors used electric cycle lamps to check tickets and give change. Cars were supposed to have their bumpers painted white to make them easier to see. There were still lots of chinks of light to be seen, the worst offenders being pubs flooding the pavement with light every time their doors opened at night. Church services, Women's Institute gatherings and other meetings were transferred to afternoons to avoid people moving about during the blackout.

Enforcing the blackout was not always easy. Lt-Col. Hamilton Pelly of The Manor at Houghton had sixty-one windows to check — not always easy, as the house was being used by several different groups.

WAR IS DECLARED

Once war was confirmed on 3 September, the population at large had few illusions about what lay ahead. Mayor W.E. Driver had this message for the people of Huntingdon:

> There will be no gains for Britain, only sacrifices. We want and ask nothing for ourselves out of this war or for others, more than peace, security, freedom and justice. We can derive some comfort from reflecting that the stand this country is taking is in accordance with all that is finest in its traditions.

Other leaders across the county echoed his sentiments.

All public entertainment and sport in the county was immediately prohibited. Church services were only to be held at the discretion of the vicar. Guidebooks were taken off the market in case of invasion (this order was not rescinded in St Ives until mid-1943, when the prospect of invasion was felt to be remote). The railways were taken over by the Ministry of Transport and used for evacuation.

Petrol rationing came into force on 22 September. Not a gallon of petrol was to be found anywhere in Huntingdonshire during the previous week. This led to a surge in demand for bicycles, and one local tradesman had an extensive waiting list of those wanting to purchase red rear lights. Coal rationing began on 1 October.

The blackout began to be seriously enforced. There were several prosecutions for infringement of the rules. Many motorists were fined for showing lights which were too bright: Mrs Phyllis Burton of Hilton, for example, was fined 3s. Conversely, numerous cyclists were fined for riding without lights. One unfortunate cyclist, Frederick Dellar from Fenstanton, was fined 10s for having a front light too bright to comply with the restrictions whilst cycling down Huntingdon High Street, and another 10s for having no rear light!

One of the greatest fears was of gas attack. Everyone, even babies, had to carry a gas mask. Hilary Usher of St Neots telephone exchange later recalled that special gas masks which incorporated a headset were provided for telephone operators. There was a nose flap which wobbled when they talked, which caused great hilarity.

Gas detector boards were erected. The boards were green: if they tarnished it was a sign of vapour gas and if they turned red this indicated the presence of liquid gas. Air-raid wardens were supplied with metal helmets, protective

The former chapel in George Street, Huntingdon, originally built in 1845, became a first-aid post during the war. (County Record Office Huntingdon: DC 132)

clothing, service respirators, rattles, handbells and whistles. The rattles would be used to signal a gas attack, ringing the handbell would signal the 'all clear'. Special yellow paint known as 'detector paint' was painted on to the tops of post boxes and on boards. This paint would change colour if a drop of blister gas in liquid form fell on it. Almost straight away some of the boards had to be moved, as they proved to be a danger to pedestrians in the blackout.

The Conservative Hall in George Street was converted into a permanent first-aid post. A wooden building with a shed at each end was erected at the end of the hall to serve as a decontamination centre. The sheds were to be used as waiting rooms. The women's entrance was on the High Street side, with the men's entrance at the other end. These entrances led into undressing rooms where top clothing would be removed and put into bins. Heavily contaminated clothing would be destroyed. From the undressing room, those contaminated would pass through an airlock into a washing room. Here all remaining clothing would be removed before using the baths provided. In the dressing room, they would be given new clothes before passing through another airlock onto the street. The back of the hall would serve as a surgery, where any casualties would be dealt with.

Ambulances and first-aid cars were on standby, mainly driven by women. These ambulances were mostly furniture vans fitted with stretchers. Forty extra beds

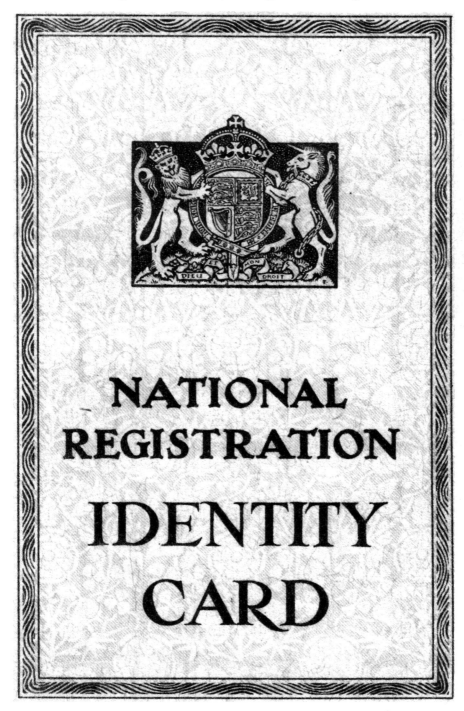

A National Registration Identity Card, belonging originally to M. Davis of Cambridge, 1943. (Cambridgeshire Collection)

were established at the County Hospital in Huntingdon, some for patients trans-
ferred from Addenbrookes in Cambridge which in turn had received cases from
London hospitals. Villages around Huntingdonshire had their own first-aid posts.
In Fenstanton, Miss A. Dawson lent a room at The Laurels in the High Street, and
Mr W. Gifford offered his van for use as an ambulance.

Large houses which had not been pressed into service for housing evacuees
or nursery children were taken over for use as hospitals. Hinchingbrooke House
became a hospital taking air-raid victims from London and, later, convalesc-
ing military patients. Conington Castle was a hostel for aged people who had
become homeless. Elton Hall was also used as an auxiliary hospital for women
patients. Any remaining houses of any size would be taken over by the military:
Great Stukeley Hall, for instance, was requisitioned and turned into an officers'
mess for the US forces at Alconbury, while at the other end of the social scale
the family business of Cross Roads Garage near Conington was requisitioned for
use by members of the 809th Engineer Aviation Battalion, who were constructing Glatton Aerodrome. Diddington Hall had an encampment of Nissen huts in
the grounds, enabling it to serve partly as an army base and partly as a military
hospital. The camp was later used for German Prisoners of War (POWs), and later
still as an American hospital, reputedly the second largest in the country. In 1945
it would also be used by the Poles as a recuperation centre.

Building air-raid shelters was a priority, but surviving County Council civil
defence files reveal arguments over public air-raid provision in 1939. Suggestions
for public-shelter locations were continually being rejected, either by the county's ARP officers or by the people living there themselves.

In St Ives, for instance, the ARP officers ruled in October 1939 that all three
suggested shelter sites were wholly unsuitable. The owner of St Ives Temperance
Hotel had herself objected to her cellar being commandeered for shelter use, as
it would seriously interfere with fuel deliveries and rubbish collection. No suitable premises could be found in St Neots at all. In Ramsey, the suggestion of the
Abbey's basement was rejected as it was too far from the town and would incon-
venience the running of the school there.

Other shelter suggestions for Ramsey, St Ives and St Neots came to nothing
due to the local high water table. Moreover, public air-raid shelter provision was
very expensive. Concrete shelters, able to accommodate up to fifty people, cost
up to £1,600 each. Home Office guidelines said that shelters should be available
for 5 per cent of the normal population, which would mean constructing six such
shelters at Fletton, three at St Ives, five at St Neots and four at Ramsey. In the end,
Huntingdonshire County Council simply decided that there would be no public
shelters at Ramsey, St Neots or St Ives, despite the large number of people visiting
these towns on Saturdays and market days.

In Godmanchester there were small public shelters in Mr Godfrey's house in
West Street and the basement of The Holme in Post Street. Huntingdon was the

only large town with adequate public shelters. In April 1940 the County ARP Emergency Committee approved three sites in the borough, namely the brewery in the High Street, the old malt house in St John's Street and No. 79 Ermine Street. Together these shelters provided safety for only about 300 people. A Huntingdon Borough report of September 1940 stated that the 'present accommodation is totally inadequate, especially on Saturdays, when there is an influx of persons from surrounding districts, estimated at between 400/500 in the afternoon and 800 in the evening'. Nor were the shelters properly managed. An inspection carried out on 2 May 1941 revealed that the keys to the brewery shelter's emergency exit door were missing (making the shelter a potential death trap), and that some of the keys to the malt house shelter were also missing.

It was clear to many observers that Huntingdonshire's ARP preparations were far from sound. Huntingdon bank clerk Philip Dickinson was an ARP warden for the early years of the war and attended a wardens' meeting on 15 November 1939. He wrote in his diary: 'In my opinion the whole thing is a farce and Heaven help Huntingdon if we ever have an air raid. We look like having a bad time of it – due to incompetence!'

Plans were put in place for caring for those whose homes had been destroyed should Huntingdonshire be bombed. Temporary shelters and feeding stations were established at Fletton, Huntingdon, Ramsey, St Ives and St Neots. Emergency stocks of food were stored at the Public Assistance Institutions in Huntingdon and St Neots. The WVS would help with cooking and serving food. On 29 September a 'census' of all households was taken to evaluate manpower and to prepare ration books. The enumerator would also write out and deliver an identity card for every person, as part of the National Registration Scheme.

It was obvious that women would have to play a greater role in the running of the county, but a proposal that a police woman should be appointed was rejected by the Joint Standing Committee, even though most of her duties would be with women and children. Revd E. O'Connor commented that: 'I cannot help thinking that the war is being exploited to carry out the ends and aims of certain women's associations.' Even as late as 1943, when some women had been appointed in city police forces for 'outdoor work', the Hunts Committee claimed that this was 'more in response to popular demand than from any prospect of their being useful.'

CHAPTER 2

'Hold at All Costs': Defending the County

As soon as war was declared, physical defence work began. Anti-tank trenches were dug around Huntingdon. Mr R.L. Fisher and a group of helpers, including women, dug the trenches in Hodge's Field, in the Newtown area, while more trenches were marked out on Mill Common and Spring Common and volunteers were sought to start digging these straight away. Trenches were also to be dug in St Peter's Road playing field and American Lane fields. Hartford residents dug trenches on the playing fields. There were also trenches dug in Ramsey, at Newtown Green, Station Road and the cricket field. These trenches were long and shallow, with sandbag shelters, those in Huntingdon being 30 yards long.

Like the blackout, the trenches could cause accidents. When returning to her home one Sunday evening in November 1939 an elderly member of the Newtown Methodist church fell into the Newtown trench. There was water in the trench at the time, but the lady's cries were fortunately soon heard and she was helped out.

This initial enthusiasm soon passed. After Dunkirk there was an appeal for volunteers to dig new trenches in Huntingdon to prevent enemy aircraft landing, but despite the fact that Lord Sandwich and the Mayor did their bit, hardly any volunteers turned up. Those that did were mainly women. However, things soon got moving and many people were soon digging for two or three hours after work. An article appeared in *The Kimboltonian* magazine describing the different techniques of the diggers in Kimbolton: some went at it like: 'a demented mechanical grab... remarkable for the lightning rapidity with which they threw up tons of earth all around themselves,' whilst others, 'after an infinitesimal amount of digging, amassed the finest collection of assorted blisters that could conveniently be contained on one pair of human hands.'

Local meadows were obstructed to prevent enemy landings. In Hemingford Abbots, poles were erected holding taut wires, with the aim of preventing enemy gliders from landing. There were concrete road blocks and barbed wire was placed at strategic locations. The concrete road blocks in Hartford were finally removed in August 1945.

Volunteers dig the foundations of new defence works around Huntingdon. (*Hunts Post*)

Trenches on their own would not stop the *Wehrmacht* though. Huntingdonshire needed armed men.

THE HOME GUARD

Minister of War, Anthony Eden, made his call to the nation for volunteers on 14 May 1940. Soon afterwards Lord Sandwich chaired a meeting at Huntingdonshire County Council, which set up the Huntingdonshire Local Defence Volunteers (LDV). By the end of the first week 800 men had enlisted for the LDV at local police stations, many of them turning up with their own guns. By the end of June there were no fewer than 2,800 men enrolled in Huntingdonshire.

At first these men were very poorly equipped, as Eric Davies of St Neots Home Guard later remembered:

This unit of very inexperienced would-be defenders of the country was placed under the command and guidance of a veteran who was a sergeant in World War One and therefore was responsible for the shotgun which was the only firearm

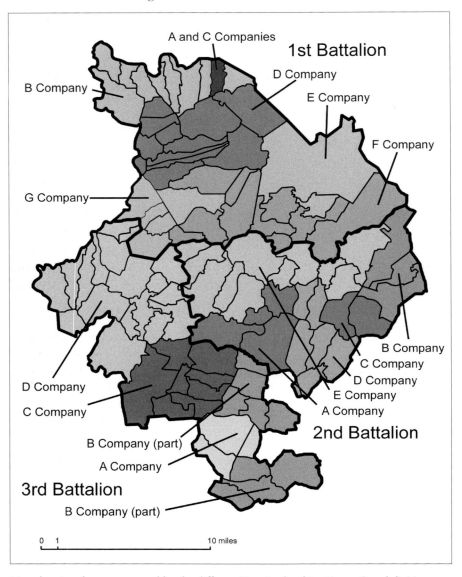

Map showing the areas covered by the different Huntingdonshire Home Guard divisions. (The authors)

available to the platoon in the initial period of the LDV... In view of the shortage of arms to equip the LDV during the critical early months, members were encouraged to arm themselves with anything that could be used to repel an invader and many recruits paraded or turned out on calls with domestic and similar articles; in fact I recall reporting at our local fortification on an invasion alert one night armed with a long bread-knife!

During September many of these men were issued with proper serge battle dress, boots and coats, and the government managed to distribute some rifles, Lewis machine-guns and grenades. Nevertheless, there were never enough guns to go round. One of the first actions undertaken by the new company commanders was to survey the exact number of shotguns available for LDV use in their area, and to ascertain from the guns' owners whether they would be happy to let other people use them. A 30-yard firing range was set up in St Ives to help with weapons training. The top brass of Huntingdonshire's Home Guard were cautious, however, and ordered that new recruits should be given 'no ammunition until such times as they are recommended by their section leader to the company commander as competent.'

By the end of 1940 the Huntingdonshire Home Guard, as it was now called, comprised 3,266 officers, NCOs and men, and was organised into three battalions. Lectures were given on all areas of warfare, including techniques of street fighting; the correct way to throw a hand grenade; the detection and prevention of espionage by enemy agents; and how to make a Molotov Cocktail, or 'Mollitoff Bottle' as it was known at the time:

A pint-sized beer bottle is best. Fill the bottle up to the shoulder only with two parts petrol, one part tar, one part kerosene oil. Shake the mixture... As some bottles will only break on very violent treatment, a small nick should be cut with a diamond or file at two places either side of the middle of the bottle... The bottle should be thrown when the flare is well alight. When the bottle breaks an immediate sheet of flame smothers everything. This flame should be fed with other Mollitoffs. A tank can easily be stalked from behind hedges and more particularly when the tank halts at a road block or for any other reason. All troops should therefore act very quickly and with great confidence.

During July and August 1941, the 2nd (East) Hunts Battalion held summer weekend training camps at Hemingford. Some training exercises went on through the night. 'All three Battalions held all-night exercises,' Col. Duberly wrote in 1944, 'and despite inclement weather during October, November and December [1941] these were always well attended and without complaint.' At one such training event in Hemingford Grey, six men were asked to demonstrate how to cross the river in full kit – denim suits, shoes, tin helmets, gas capes, dummy respirators and rifles slung across their backs. The men, all volunteers, refused to use a lifeline as the exercise had been performed elsewhere. They began to cross from the Wyton side, at a point where the river was 90ft wide and 10ft deep. Unfortunately, two of the men, Leslie Borson (aged thirty-three) and Eric Moore (seventeen) were drowned. These camps continued to be held though – another series of eight weekend training camps was held in 1943 at Godmanchester Common and Hemingford Abbots.

Group photograph of the St Ives Home Guard, at camp during the Second World War.
(Norris Museum: PH/S.IVE/People/40)

Training with live ammunition was necessary but very dangerous. Grenade training for the 3rd (South) Hunts Battalion was carried out at Little Paxton gravel pits. In one incident a live grenade was accidentally dropped on the ground and the trainee and his instructor only had a couple of seconds to jump into the safety trench before it exploded, covering them both with earth and bits of sandbag. On another occasion a trainee was being instructed in how to use a Thompson sub-machine-gun on its single-fire setting inside St Neots Drill Hall. Unfortunately the trainee engaged the gun's automatic setting, and he lost control of the gun due to its powerful recoil, emptying the entire magazine and leaving a series of bullet holes in the roof. Another man literally shot himself in the foot when he dropped his Sten gun. He spent a week in Papworth Hospital.

PREPARING FOR INVASION

Every village and town in Huntingdonshire had its own Invasion Committee, made up of Home Guard commanders, a food organiser, ARP and first-aid personnel. The duty of the committee was to plan and prepare for the anticipated German attacks, but in practice it tended to act as a forum for sorting out local problems and disputes between the military and civilian authorities. Surprisingly there was no obligation on the individual Invasion Committees to coordinate with their neighbours. It was 'recommended' that they talk to each other, but it was not until July 1942 that an overall 'County Invasion Committee' was set up, under the chairmanship of the Earl of Sandwich. One Invasion Committee refused to allow Home Guard members to attend meetings in uniform in case it created panic.

The village Invasion Committees were not expected to provide any armed defence should the Germans invade, but were instead tasked with ensuring that the necessities of life – water, food, and communications – should be safeguarded as much as possible during any fighting. They would ensure that the community would live on its own resources and function as a self-contained unit until it was relieved. They would organise the food supply, deal with casualties and refugees, and ensure that the 'stand firm' policy was maintained.

Every village had to identify alternative supplies of fresh water should its main wells be bombed out, as well as to list all the main tools and mechanical equip-ment in its area, and had to create an efficient messenger service. This last duty was supposed to be carried out by young boys and girls, riding through the fighting on bicycles. In 1943 the Huntingdonshire County Invasion Committee clarified that these messengers should ideally be aged sixteen or over, and that fourteen-year-old children should only be used if there really was no one else available. There was no money to provide bicycles – the messengers would be expected to use their own. There was no money for maps, either, and it was recommended that each village drew up a map on its own, and paste it to the village hall wall.

Although Huntingdonshire's villagers were not expected to shoot at Germans, they were still expected to delay any German advance, by blocking roads, build-ing earth walls, digging trenches and so on. Instructions were sent to every village

Surviving pillbox, north of Ramsey. (The authors)

on how to dig a 'slit trench,' which was very narrow, only 2ft at the widest point, and which gave a high degree of protection against artillery fire or attacks from Stuka dive-bombers. The villagers were not supposed to dig them until the invasion was imminent – the trenches would get wet and possibly dangerous if they were dug too early – but they certainly were expected to mark out the routes of the trenches and gather together corrugated-iron sheets for additional defence. 'Care should be taken to have a garden spade available when required,' the official pamphlet solemnly stated.

Huntingdonshire's towns, however, had to prepare for real fighting. In May 1942 Huntingdon Borough Council issued a booklet to every household giving advice about what to do if invading German forces tried to attack the town. 'When the time comes, civil defence workers and others… must fight in close defence of the town or village; in streets and houses, with bomb, bayonet, tommy gun, molotov cocktail, etc.'

As there would not be enough soldiers to mount a proper perimeter defence of each town, the Home Guard's combat plans were instead based on the concept of each town having a smaller 'keep' area, which would be defended to the end by local soldiers, and for which no withdrawal orders would ever be given. In St Ives, for instance, the keep area was defined as being on the south side of the river bridge (and therefore, in reality, in the parish of Hemingford Grey). This area included the junction where the railway trestle line crossed the New Bridges, so it was a crucial spot to defend. The keep's headquarters was stationed in the Dolphin Inn. In the event of German attack this area would be defended by seventy-five men from 'C' Company 2nd Hunts Battalion Home Guard, tasked with the object of denying both the road and railway crossings over the river Ouse to the German army. Another platoon of thirty men was stationed next to the part of the railway viaduct which lay to the east of St Ives and there was a further mobile reserve of another thirty soldiers based in the Broadway in the town centre, but the men in these platoons could withdraw if ordered to do so. The keep's troops were not so fortunate: 'The keep defence area at St Ives will be held at all costs,' according to the Home Guard's defence scheme, 'and under no circumstances will the garrison withdraw'.

As a last resort, the Home Guard planned to detonate explosives under St Ives's medieval bridge. 'We were told that if the enemy came we had to destroy all papers at Headquarters and retreat over the bridge, which would be blown up,' one former Home Guard member recalled.

Huntingdon's defence was organised around two keeps. The first was centred on the medieval bridge between Huntingdon and Godmanchester, as it was recognised that a successful river crossing would be one of the invaders' main military objectives. Defence of the bridge was entrusted to the 100 men of No.4 (Godmanchester) Platoon, 'A' Company of the 2nd Hunts Battalion Home Guard – under the command of Lt J. Looker. Guns would be positioned in the

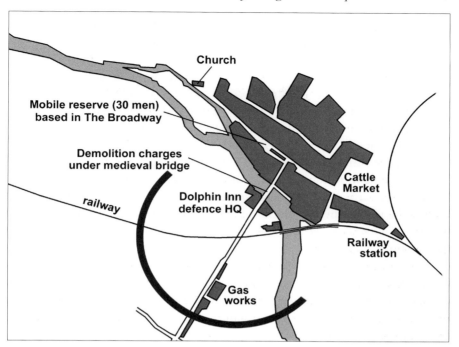

Map showing how the Home Guard planned to defend St Ives. The semi-circular line shows the boundary of the 'keep'; the Germans were expected to march northwards towards this area. (The authors)

Possibly a Home Guard shooting team, photographed in August 1942. (Norris Museum: PH/S.IVE/People/16)

hosiery mill, in Mill House garden, in Godmanchester's railway station and sid-
ings, and on Castle Hill itself, all having the objective of preventing German tanks
from pushing northwards into the town. The men guarding the medieval bridge
were expected to fight 'at all costs and under no circumstances will there be any
withdrawal.' Although the plan does not explicitly say as much, it is reasonable to
assume that Huntingdon's medieval bridge would have been blown up to prevent
its use by German forces, in the same way as the bridge at St Ives.

Huntingdon's second keep was the area around North Station and Brampton
Road, and the Home Guard's intention was to defend this area with eighty men of
No.1 (Huntingdon) Platoon, based in the new grammar school buildings (where
Scholar's Avenue is today). The purpose of this area's defence was to prevent the
German army capturing the mainline railway station. In addition, there was a
smaller force of forty men based in the former workhouse on St Peter's Road,
who were supposed to 'delay, harass and inflict the greatest loss' on German forces
by defending the iron bridge over Ermine Street, but this locality was not expected
to be defended to the death. If German attacks proved too strong then the troops
at the iron bridge would be ordered to withdraw to the North Station keep. A
similar group of soldiers based at the Model Laundry on Hartford Road, guarding
the way into the town from St Ives, would fall back onto the bridge keep if necessary. Finally, there was a mobile reserve of forty-five men, based at Riverside, 'from
where it will be used for reinforcing or for counter-attack purposes.'

Just how realistic were these plans? Huntingdon could call on 305 men for
its Home Guard defence, but they had only thirty-four machine-guns between
them. The North Station keep, for instance, had just thirteen automatic weapons
for its eighty men. The majority of these weapons were the Spigot mortar, which
was a low-mounted anti-tank weapon, and the American Lewis gun, a gas-pow-
ered light machine-gun which had been used to arm some British tanks in the
First World War but which was obsolete even by 1920s standards. The grammar
school buildings off Brampton Road would be defended by two Lewis guns. A
nest of one Lewis gun and one Spigot mortar would be placed on the Brampton
Road allotments, another Spigot would fire from the window of Warren's bunga-
low on Brampton Road and other guns were dotted here and there in ones and
twos. The North Station keep could also call on two Northover projectors, which
launched grenades with the aid of caps from a toy pistol and which looked like 'a
large drainpipe mounted on twin legs.'

The Bridge keep had even fewer modern guns, just eight, to share among 100
men. A Spigot mortar and a Lewis gun would fire on the Germans from the
windows of the hosiery mill, while two Spigots would guard the railway station
and two Lewis guns would be placed in the garden of Mill House. The remaining
mortar and Lewis gun would be positioned on Castle Hill itself, which would
be the first time the site of the Norman castle had been armed since 1645. The
'counter-attack' mobile force at Riverside had, even as late as January 1943, been

Albert Edward Wayman, GNR and LNER timekeeper, next to the sandbag defences outside his cabin north-east of Huntingdon railway bridge. This photograph was taken during the winter of 1940. (Mike Stephenson)

Gun emplacement on Huntingdon railway bridge. (County Record Office Huntingdon: 1096/109)

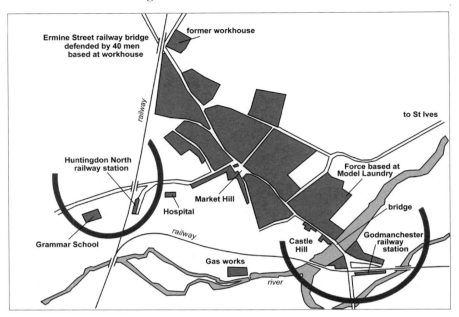

Map showing how the Home Guard planned to defend Huntingdon. The two semi-circular lines indicate the boundaries of the 'keeps', areas which would be defended at all costs. The force based at the former workhouse in St Peter's Road and the similar force based at the Model Laundry could be called upon to support the keeps if necessary. (The authors)

allocated no modern weapons at all. Its troops would have to do with makeshift home-made weapons, ancient family guns, or agricultural shotguns.

Huntingdonshire's Home Guard made as many preparations as it could, in the hope that more weapons might turn up if the Germans really invaded. It is doubtful whether any determined German advance could have been halted. The Germans used *Blitzkrieg* tactics, where huge quantities of modern assault weapons were concentrated in a just a small number of fast-moving individual attacks, separated from each other by miles and miles of uninvaded territory where nothing happened at all. A *Blitzkrieg* attack looked, on a map, rather like the prongs of a fork. If Huntingdonshire fell between the prongs of a German invasion then they would not see any fighting at all, but would after time become completely encircled. If on the other hand Huntingdonshire was situated exactly upon one of the prongs then it is hard to see how the local Home Guard could have delayed the Germans. A full *Blitzkrieg* attack, involving literally hundreds of modern Panzer tanks, Stuka dive-bombers, and German soldiers – hardened by their experiences on the Eastern Front against Russia – would have made short work of the county's defences.

In reality a proper defence could only have been managed with units from the regular army, but no one knew how to incorporate that into their planning. The defence scheme for Huntingdon assumed that: 'RAF regiments and any regular army details stationed in the town at the time of the emergency would undoubtedly be available to assist in defence'. The defence scheme for St Ives was less optimistic, explicitly stating that 'it is not anticipated that any further military assistance will be available.'

TESTING THE DEFENCES

The surviving records of invasion exercises reveal interesting assumptions made about the speed of a likely German advance and about the likelihood of just how successful Huntingdonshire's defence would be. In every respect the Home Guard seems to have been brutally realistic about their own chances, or rather their lack of them.

In St Neots, for example, a combined invasion exercise was carried out on 24 June 1942. The background assumption to the exercise was that German forces had invaded the north Norfolk coast on 20 June. (In itself this was a reasonable assumption to make, as the German army had successfully invaded Norway in 1940, and if the Germans could use Denmark as a base to attack Norway then there was every chance they could also use it as a base to attack England's vulnerable East Anglian coastline.) In just five days, according to the exercise, the German army had overrun Norfolk and Suffolk. German airborne troops were assumed to have captured Bourn and Oakington Airfields on 23 June, using the bases for their own aircraft. It was also assumed that the Germans would be pushing south-west, aiming for the crossings over the river Ouse. The role of St Neots Home Guard was to prevent this. How long could they hold out?

The answer was just under three hours. The exercise on 24 June had the 'German' forces begin their entry into the town at 8.30 p.m. By 11.00 p.m. the bridge had been captured and the exercise was over.

A similar combined invasion exercise was carried out in Huntingdon on 27 September 1942. This exercise assumed that the Germans had landed in Norfolk six days earlier. By midday on 26 September the frontline ran from March across to Ely and down to Newmarket. By midnight the Germans were on the outskirts of Peterborough, and had occupied Chatteris, Ramsey, and the strategically important river crossings at Earith. Dawn of 27 September saw the Germans begin their attack on Peterborough, overrun RAF Warboys, attack RAF Wyton and occupy St Ives and Fenstanton. 'German' troops were spotted on the Great North Road at Alconbury Hill. Huntingdon's Home Guard's objective was to deny the river crossing to the enemy, but to try to keep it open for British armed forces.

These exercises were planned to be as realistic as possible, within limits. Live ammunition could not be used, obviously, but blanks were used in rifles, and

Soldiers on a machine-gun post. (Cambridgeshire Libraries: T.G.K4 32761)

'cracker blanks' simulated the sounds of machine-gun fire. Members of the military often let off smoke bombs or detonated loud 'thunder flashes.' Mines were represented by little cardboard discs placed on the ground, while road or railway blocks were indicated by painted white lines or trails of sawdust. Official umpires, wearing white armbands or displaying white crosses on their car windscreens, watched all the proceedings, took notes and wrote detailed reports later on how the exercise had gone. They were exciting events to watch. 'I saw a whole troop of soldiers in Cambridge Street in Godmanchester spend most of the day attacking and defending a pink coloured large ruined house,' I.B. Hunter later remembered. 'Guns were blazing and no holds were barred, although I do recognise now that the Army were firing blanks!'

In Huntingdon, machine-gun fire was heard during the 'Battle of Ingram Street'. The local newspaper reported that:

> … with frequent explosions and flashes, belching clouds of smoke, fire engines and ambulances racing through the streets and certain roads closed to traffic, the scene at Huntingdon was as realistic as it could possibly be. The town was theoretically 'blitzed' and immense damage was done.

In June 1942, the Home Guard in Ramsey held a 'realistic' exercise in which the Great Eastern mills were attacked by the men of Ramsey Forty Foot, Mereside, the Hollow and St Mary's, while the buildings were defended by the Ramsey Home Guard. The use of thunder flashes caused some local residents to fear they were genuinely under attack.

Occasionally the RAF joined in the exercises, playing the part of German dive-bombers to add more realism to the activities. An ARP exercise in Somersham on 19 April 1942 was buzzed by a low-flying RAF aeroplane. The exercise's umpire wrote that it was 'a real test, it gave all personnel an idea of what real blitz conditions would be like, and how difficult first aid work would be when being dive-bombed at the same time.' At times the realism even extended to dressing up 'enemy' troops in German uniforms, a risky practice during wartime, one would have thought. For the 'Buzz IV' exercise, held in April 1944, German linguists were dressed in enemy uniforms and were instructed to speak no other language.

Later the Americans joined in the training. In one exercise at USAAF Molesworth, the 3rd (South) Hunts Battalion Home Guard was pretending to attack the base. Eric Davies later recalled:

> This event developed in a rather disconcerting way for the platoon members who, after having advanced to cover in a ditch on the outskirts of the airfield and were planning the final attack to 'sabotage' some of the aircraft, were startled to find that they were under fire from two 'Flying Fortresses', and worse still, live .45 ammunition was being fired over their heads from the machine guns of the planes.

The Americans invited the Home Guard soldiers into the base's bar afterwards to calm their nerves. This incident was tactfully omitted from the Battalion Colonel's summary of the exercise, which concentrated instead on the Home Guard's successful smokescreen-covered attack and the final assault on the airfield's buildings.

Hardly any place in Huntingdonshire was left untouched by these exercises, even villages were caught up. The main lesson of these exercises and others like them, was to reveal the utter confusion of command. In an exercise at Kimbolton on 11 October 1942, for example, the army forgot to inform the civilian participants about the chemical constitution of the smoke bombs they were using. People were taken to hospital suffering from strange respiratory problems for which the nurses had no treatment. They had been expecting eyesight problems from tear gas instead.

Communications were poor all round. The report on the St Ives combined invasion exercise, held on 20 September 1942, said: 'Wardens could give more information to the Military, and the Military should keep Civil Defence on the spot better posted with the position of the enemy, etc. This information would have prevented many Civil Defence workers from becoming casualties'. Strategy changed too: 'Many times has it been necessary to alter the perimeters through changes in higher command, necessitating the laying of miles and miles of dannert and barbed wire, only later to collect it all again,' commented one person after the war.

LIFE IN THE HOME GUARD

When they were not exercising, members of the Huntingdonshire Home Guard acted as guides around the county to regular army armoured divisions, as all signposts had been removed. They also manned checkpoints at certain vital roads. No one was let through until they showed proof of identity. The Home Guard also ran a pigeon service, delivering messages. They laid miles of barbed wire at strategic points.

It was not all hard work though. The St Neots and District Home Guard ran a darts league. There were regular shooting matches between different Home Guard units and between the Home Guard and the police, as well as football matches and all types of sporting contests. Members of the Great Gransden Home Guard even had a shooting match against King Peter of Yugoslavia when he visited his mother Queen Marie, who was living at Mill House.

Attendance, however, was taken seriously. One Home Guard member in Stibbington was fined for not attending parades. In 1943 a Ramsey Home Guard member narrowly escaped a prison sentence for attending only nine out of twenty parades.

Despite the threat of attack, there were still those who were reluctant to 'do their bit'. A letter in the *Hunts Post* complained of the 'appalling lethargy' in Godmanchester regarding recruitment into the Home Guard. An editorial in the same paper put it even more strongly:

> It is quite incredible that at a moment… when the whole fate of the civilised world for generations to come hangs by the merest thread, there should exist men who still decline to take their fair share of the burdens which fall upon us as a nation. While the Home Guard and Civil Defence services cry out for volunteers, there are slackers in this county who do absolutely nothing in the sphere of national service. It is a position which is rapidly becoming intolerable.

GENUINE GERMANS

It is commonly thought that, due to the absence of any actual German invasion, the Home Guard had no direct contact with the enemy. But the Germans parachuted a large number of spies into England during the Battle of Britain period, and there was a always a real chance that local Home Guard volunteers would encounter an enemy combatant.

On Saturday 1 February 1941, Cpl H. Godfrey of the Ramsey Home Guard Company, commanded by Capt. H. Newton, captured an enemy secret agent complete with radio transmitter and other equipment. He wore civilian clothes beneath his flying suit and carried about £500 in English money and food,

Members of the Home Guard on parade, probably at Ramsey Heights. (Cambridgeshire Libraries: Y.Ram.K4 12565)

Surviving pillbox next to Bodsey Bridge, north of Ramsey. (The authors)

including a German sausage and a flask of brandy. Local farm workers spotted him after he had hurt his ankle, and reported him to fellow farm worker Cpl Harry Godfrey. The spy, Josef Jakobs, a German national, had a British identity card and ration book but the tags in his clothing were in German. He was escorted to London by Inspector Horace Jenkins of the Ramsey Police. Jakobs was tried and in August 1941 he was executed at the Tower of London, the first spy to be shot in Britain during the war. The chair in which he was shot remained on display in the Tower for some years.

On Sunday 4 May 1941 men of the 3rd (South) Hunts Battalion were called upon to search for and capture four Germans who had baled out of their crashing bomber. All four were apprehended, two just outside the county boundary. The Germans had been unlucky enough to crash on the same day as a full Home Guard exercise.

St Neots Home Guard operated an anti-aircraft installation on the roof of Little Barford power station, comprising four machine-guns bolted together and controlled by a single trigger. Eric Davies later recalled:

> I did, in fact, once open fire on a low-flying German plane crossing over the Power Station, although it may have been my wishful thinking, the aircraft seemed to waver and I have always liked to wonder if I can claim a hit and the subsequent destruction of the enemy bomber before it reached base.

What cannot be denied is the bravery of Huntingdonshire's men in contemplating the possibility of German forces attacking their towns and villages. When he visited Hemingford Park on 17 September 1944, Gen. Finch spoke in honour of Huntingdonshire's Home Guard: 'These are the men who would have fought nobly, and to the death, if Hitler's men had invaded our land.'

CHAPTER 3

'Huntingdonshire Invaded': Evacuees

Being a rural county, Huntingdonshire was expected to house evacuees from the cities. As early as January 1939 plans were being made to inspect homes for evacuation and a room was hired at the Norris Library in St Ives to administer the Government's evacuation scheme. The Mayor of Huntingdon, Councillor W.E. Driver, wrote to all households:

> I am sure it needs no words of mine to convey to you what your help will mean to the children of those big cities and I have every confidence in the people of Huntingdon playing their full part in assisting this national effort for the provision of their safety.

Huntingdonshire's proximity to London would make it easy to transport large numbers out of the capital, and well over 10,000 evacuees were expected. A booklet was issued by the WVS giving instructions to those who would receive evacuees. Householders would receive a payment of 10s 6d for one child, or 8s 6d per child if taking more than one. This was to cover full board and lodging, but not clothes or medical expenses. Evacuees would not be bringing bedding with them, but extra blankets could be obtained from the local authority.

THE FIRST ARRIVALS

The evacuation began on Friday 1 September 1939. The first train arrived at 9.55 a.m., carrying girls from Highbury and Tollington Park. A second train arrived at 10.45 a.m. and another, carrying younger children, at 4.20 p.m.

Mr W.T. Carter, headmaster of Brampton School, was in charge of the arrangements and issued instructions through a megaphone. The children filed across the bridge over the railway and were met by members of the men's and women's Voluntary Aid Detachment (VAD). They marched out of the station and across the road, which had been roped off, onto Mill Common. Temporary latrines

HUNTS. POST, THURSDAY, SEPTEMBER 7, 1939

CHILDREN INVADE HUNTINGDONSHIRE

Arrival of the first train load of evacuated children from London on Friday at Huntingdon North Station.   In the centre is Mr. W. T. Carter (headmaster of Brampton School) with megaphone, directing the children where to go to receive rations before boarding the waiting buses to convey them to the villages.

Evacuees arriving in Huntingdon. (*Hunts Post*)

had been erected. The line of children passed through the food tent where Mr N. Armstrong, headmaster of Huntingdon Grammar School, was in charge as rations officer and assisted by other grammar school staff and pupils. Evacuees were given a carrier bag and passed along a line of tables where they received tins of corned beef, sweetened and unsweetened milk, two packets of biscuits and ¼lb of chocolate. After collecting their rations the children were given a mug of water from the tap which had been installed by the county surveyor – many of those who arrived in the afternoon had not had a drink since they had left London at 8.00 a.m. Lord Sandwich himself was present when the first train arrived. Lady Sandwich, inspecting the arrangements in the food tent, was mistaken for one of the teachers and offered the usual rations.

The *Hunts Post* reported: 'It was pathetic to see the little children bowed down by the weight of their pillowcases and haversacks which contained a change of clothing, gym shoes and a day's supply of food. Each child had three identity labels attached to their clothing.'

In one case, a girl of thirteen was in charge of her brothers and sisters – seven altogether. Some of the younger children were tearful, but they soon cheered up and when they walked away from the station they began singing. Some of the children were so thrilled at being in a field that they danced and raced around in it. One girl fainted, but she was soon looked after by ambulance men. The children were marshalled to a line of buses and then sent to various towns and villages across the county.

On Saturday 2 September more trains arrived, this time carrying mothers with babies and expectant mothers. These had more luggage, so the transfer to buses took longer. Many Huntingdon women, as well as scouts and girl guides, were on hand to help. One waiting room on the station was turned into a first-aid post. The officials from London commented on the excellence of the arrangements.

One boy evacuated from London became separated from his classmates. On Sunday 3 September Philip Dickinson wrote in his diary that:

> … on Saturday evening Hillary brought home a small boy whose name was Tommy Davis and he lived at 255 Sussex Way Hornsey Road, N4. He had missed his proper train and had been waiting patiently from 2 p.m. till 7 p.m. for instruction as to what he was to do. My wife took pity on him and brought him home and he stayed with us.

Tommy did not have to stay with the Dickinsons for long, as on the following Monday he was 'fetched today at 10.30 a.m. by Mrs Bailey who took him to his school which had been located at Warboys.' Tommy Davis's mother wrote a letter of gratitude to Mrs Dickinson.

By Sunday morning, some 6,000 evacuees had been received at Huntingdon. They came from Haringey, Hornsey, Tottenham, Tollington and Highbury Vale, and were sent to St Ives, Ramsey, Somersham, Warboys, Leighton, Abbots Ripton, Brampton and Godmanchester. Two more trains were expected on Sunday, but news came through that the evacuation from London had stopped.

At St Neots railway station 300 children arrived on the Friday. Most were sent to Eynesbury. The only train which arrived in St Neots on Saturday was one which should have stopped at Biggleswade and had to be sent back. No children at all arrived in St Neots on Saturday, despite the fact that large numbers of helpers were waiting for them at the station. St Neots itself had only twenty-four evacuated children who had arrived on Friday. Things went slightly better in Eaton Socon where 600 children were received. One five year old went missing, but was quickly recovered. The children appeared to regard the trip as an unexpected holiday.

A group of 240 children and twenty-six adults from Finsbury Park and Highbury Vale was transferred from Huntingdon Station to St Ives. They were taken to the Corn Exchange and given tea and biscuits by the WVS and other helpers. The children were soon sent off to their new homes, some travelling in cars which had been offered by the helpers. They too thought it was like a holiday, as the *Hunts Post* commented: 'To these innocent youngsters it was all part of a grand holiday and they were fortunately unable to comprehend the grave underlying circumstances which were causing their evacuation.'

Feeding those who were to be billeted in empty and partly furnished houses proved a problem in St Ives. A party of forty-two was fed at the Golden Lion and another twenty-five at the Temperance Hotel. On Monday the WVS began providing meals at the Corn Exchange and, by Tuesday, 127 mothers and children were eating there. Some of the evacuees in St Ives were refugee children who could speak no English.

Grammar school pupil, Pat Whitney, handing out water to evacuees arriving at Huntingdon Station, 1939. (*Hunts Post*)

The evacuees being led to their buses. (*Hunts Post*)

The first contingent of evacuees arrived in Ramsey on Sunday, comprising about 400 individuals from Islington, Holloway and other parts of North London. Mothers and children arrived in Ramsey, although only children had been expected. They were given tea and biscuits at the old schools before going to their billets. Around sixty mothers and children went to Ramsey Heights.

Brampton welcomed 313 children and expectant mothers. The village's small school was used as a social centre. Buckden received 200 boys from a secondary school in Muswell Hill, together with the full staff of twenty-three teachers and four helpers. Around 200 boys and twenty masters from Highbury County School arrived at Kimbolton. They were received at Mandeville Hall before being taken to their new homes. On Saturday they played a cricket match in the park, and a special service for them was held in the parish church on Sunday afternoon. Evacuees at Pidley came from Tottenham and at Ellington forty evacuees arrived from Haringey.

Other villages also took in groups of evacuees: Abbotsley received fifty children and five teachers; Catworth took in thirty children, one teacher and three helpers; Covington twenty children, two teachers and one helper; Eynesbury Hardwicke eighteen children and two teachers; Great Gransden sixty children and six teachers; Hail Weston sixty children and six teachers, Offord Cluny and Darcy sixty children, six teachers and two helpers; Southoe and Middloe forty-eight children, two teachers and two helpers, Great Staughton 120 children and twelve teachers; Stow Longa twenty children, one teacher and two helpers; Tilbrook forty children and four teachers; Warboys had 500 evacuees and Waresley fifty children and five teachers.

The Offords' evacuees were told to stand in the church rooms in the village so that they could be 'selected' by those villagers who had promised to take children. 'The last poor soul left standing in the church rooms must have felt terribly unwanted', comments the official history of the village.

Many people went out of their way to welcome the evacuees. One bachelor in Godmanchester gave up his whole house except one room to house twenty children. Another man, Mr Watson, gave up his house to Lady Reading's Sun Ray Nursery which had transferred from London. There were ninety-two children aged between two and three, all in need of special care. Mr Watson went to live in Cambridge. Hinchingbrooke House was also given over to a nursery school from Canning Town: a group of seventy-two children aged between two and five were expected, but some did not arrive straight away because their mothers were hop picking in Kent.

Col. Barrie Goldie CBE placed the Old Rectory at Brampton at the disposal of the authorities, as did Mr J.B. Kelly, clerk to the county council, with his house at Mill Common in Huntingdon. Alconbury House and Brampton Park were also offered by their owners. By the following week, 100 children and twenty staff from the Shoreditch Nursery were in residence at Brampton Park and Edward

House. When the Duchess of Gloucester visited Edward House in May 1940, the children were dressed in pink and green smocks for the occasion.

Another forty infants from the Tottenham Day Nursery were at Alconbury House. Paxton Park School was taken over to accommodate fifty expectant mothers, whose children were cared for at The Holme, Godmanchester. In 1940 The Holme was home to children from the Docklands settlement. Riverlea in Godmanchester was used to accommodate the Stratford day nursery, while The Grove became a home for 'difficult children'. Offord Darcy Rectory was used to house invalids and the disabled. Mrs G. Jones lent her house, Greystones in Ramsey, as a sick bay for unaccompanied evacuee children. It would have sixteen beds and the Red Cross would supply nurses when necessary. The Garden House hotel at Norman Cross was later used for a similar purpose.

Immediate arrangements were put in place to cope with the large numbers of extra residents who had to be fed, educated and looked after. It was decided that schools would not reopen for at least a week whilst plans were finalised.

The organisation required to pull off Huntingdonshire's evacuation operation was huge, and in general it ran smoothly. Twenty buses were used: the double-deckers covered 566½ miles and the single-deckers 1,034 miles, in a total of sixty-two journeys carrying 2,439 passengers. Miss Ling, the organiser of the Huntingdon National Services Committee, was responsible for the payment of allowances to 'officially evacuated' adults. They had to produce an official government form, as those who had come of their own accord to a 'place of safety' were not to be included. The evacuation arrangements seem to have run like clockwork in rural areas.

LIFE FOR THE EVACUEES

Not everyone welcomed the evacuees. The Mayor of Huntingdon, reported that:

> I regret to say that at two houses one of our officers was insulted and, to make it worse, in front of these tired people… we who live in a fairly safe area can surely best show our good fortune by helping those who, through no fault of their own, come from dangerous areas.

Many people complained at the cost of keeping evacuees. They thought of it as 'town children' having a holiday in the country which their parents did not have to pay for. Bad feeling was caused in Warboys when a house was rejected by a schoolmaster for use by his pupils because it had no water supply. Appeals for clothes and other items were often met with the reply, 'parents should provide them', but they were desperately needed, particularly as 'town shoes' did not stand up well to country living. In May 1940, Huntingdonshire saw the first prosecution for refusing to take an evacuee. Walter Dunkley, a decorator from Brenton Villas, Brampton, was asked to take a nine-year-old boy who had been in Brampton for seven months, but who needed a new billet. Dunkley refused and left the boy at the billeting office. He was fined £2: the boy later returned to London.

There was bad feeling between villages such as Old Weston, which had sixty or seventy children, and neighbouring Leighton, which had none. Some people stated that they were willing to go to gaol rather than take any more evacuees. These included one woman who had taken in three women and ten children. One of the women had left without paying any board and another had taken a pram and some blankets away with her when she left.

There were those who resented the influx or mistreated those in their care. One Bluntisham woman was sentenced to three months hard labour for beating an eight-year-old evacuee with a stick. Huntingdon resident Philip Dickinson was unimpressed by the behaviour of some of the schoolgirl evacuees. 'These two evacuees went to a dance organised by their school in the evening and arrived home at 10 p.m.,' he wrote on 4 November 1939:

> Apparently they all took 'boys' which they had picked up in the streets. Questioning the girls afterwards showed that most of the 'boys' which attended were not properly known and were the result of promiscuous wandering up and down the High Street and 'getting off.' It is a disgusting and disgraceful state of affairs that young girls of thirteen and fourteen should be encouraged by their school to do such things.

Lucy Boston returned home to Hemingford Grey one evening to find a woman and a toddler on her doorstep:

> They came from the East End and had already been sitting outside an empty house for some time, having spent the previous night lying like sardines on the floor of some church hall in St Ives. No one had told us to expect them or I would have had some welcome ready for them, however great my reluctance and fear.

Nevertheless, Mrs Lilley and her son were soon made welcome at the Manor House. Lucy Boston soon heard of other evacuees whose new homes were not so happy. One London family, evacuated to a large house in St Ives, was forbidden from using the front or back doors and had to climb in through the windows instead. In another instance a mother with two children in St Ives was given an unheated attic, a bedstead with no bedding, and ordered not to use the kitchen.

Some evacuees were treated so poorly that they moved back to London, to take their chances with the German bombs. Boredom was another problem. Many of the evacuees billeted in Hemingford Abbots, for example, returned to the capital because they found the village too quiet and there was no evening entertainment.

Lucy Boston, at home in Hemingford Grey. (Cambridgeshire Libraries)

In October, three boys, one aged twelve and two aged thirteen, were found sleeping under a car in Alconbury. They had run away from their billets in Elton and were returning to London. When questioned, they replied, 'We like our billets, but we are returning to London because we cannot go to the pictures every day.'

In April 1941, one boy arrived among a party of thirty evacuees at St Neots. He claimed to have been evacuated ten times, and to have run away each time. Later in the war, in January 1944, two evacuees from the St Neots area were caught in Sandy: they had stolen two RAF bicycles and were planning to cycle back home to London.

Others welcomed children into their homes. Miss Enid Hunt from St Ives was mentioned in a national newspaper for caring for a minimum of fifteen evacuees (sometimes more) throughout the war years. They were all boys, from the Lewisham area. She did all the cooking, washing and mending herself. Miss Hunt took all the boys to the Free church every Sunday and regularly visited the bathing place in St Ives with them in summer. The evacuees themselves, in most cases, did their best to adapt to the strange way of life in the countryside. Kathleen Jones, billeted with Mrs Bowyer at Crossways in Brampton, recalled her time there as 'the best four years of my life'. Schools put on plays and held sports days and prize-givings – in fact they tried to carry on as normal. They also tried to repay the kindnesses they had received from local people. For example, pupils from Montern Street LCC School invited their foster parents at Warboys to a film show on the school projector as a way of showing their appreciation. Locals reciprocated by putting on parties and outings to the cinema for the evacuees. Almost every village held Christmas parties for the evacuees. The children from Gillespie Road Infants School in London, billeted in St Neots, were given tea in Eynesbury church rooms. The tea included a 'mammoth cake' given by Mrs Schofield, the mother of one of the London children. There were free shows in the local cinemas for both evacuees and local children.

In St Ives, the upper room of the Free church school was allocated as a social centre for the teachers who had accompanied the evacuees. The large schoolroom below would be used as a rest room for mothers with young children. The Slepe Hall playing fields were offered for use by the London children. Special Jewish services were held at the Free church for more than twenty Jewish evacuees who were living in St Ives.

Huntingdon's Trinity church schoolroom was converted into a social centre for the evacuees. As many as forty women started to gather there to write letters, read, knit, sew or play cards. Books and magazines were donated by local people. Another part of the building was used as a crèche. There were organised games on Wednesdays and Fridays, a piano and a stage, which was used for dancing.

Social centres were set up in the smaller towns and villages, too. The Constitutional Hall in Fenstanton was open daily as a rest and reading room. Ramsey Parish Room provided a club for girls over the age of twelve on Mondays and Wednesdays. The Vestry chapel at Ellington was also set up as a recreation room for evacuated children once blackout arrangements had been made. Elsewhere across the county, clubs and centres were being opened. Mrs Adams of Little Stukeley allowed the use of her bathroom two mornings a week to help out foster parents and allow evacuees to take hot baths.

Communal feeding centres soon became necessary, as many mothers with children were living in empty houses with no cooking facilities. Volunteers were cooking for 130–145 people a day at the Corn Exchange in St Ives. On one evening alone, when 600 evacuees were due to arrive, 10,067 sausages were cooked on two ordinary household cookers. By November 1940 the St Ives kitchen was producing three lunch sittings daily. Soon the feeding centre at the Corn Exchange was also providing Kosher meals for Jewish evacuees. The welcome received by the Jewish refugees in St Ives was much appreciated, and a letter of thanks from the Rabbi was published, on behalf of the children:

… who at so early a period in their lives have tasted the bitter fruit of racial and religious persecution. In an age where intolerance is so rampant and insensate hatred knows no leash, an attitude such as you have adopted and such selfless assistance as you have given does much to restore one's faith in the goodness of mankind and the ultimate return on the part of all peoples to the paths of sanity.

Christmas party at Huntingdon Day Nursery, 30 December 1943. (*Hunts Post*)

HUNTS. POST, THURSDAY, DECEMBER 5, 1940

GOVERNMENT VISITOR EATS SEVENPENNY LUNCH AT HUNTINGDON

Mr Geoffrey Shakespeare, Minister of Health, enjoying a 7*d* lunch at the communal feeding centre at Trinity church schoolroom, Huntingdon, 1940. (*Hunts Post*)

In fact everyone using the Corn Exchange canteen was full of praise for its facilities. One evacuee lady even suggested that a statue of the supervisor, Mrs R.G. Parker, should be placed in Market Hill in place of the Oliver Cromwell monument. People were walking in from Hemingford, Fenstanton and Needingworth to get a hot dinner at the Corn Exchange. In the early days all the cooking was done on three small gas stoves. It was not until the middle of 1942 that there was a sink with a water supply over it. Most of the cooking was done by the same volunteers, week after week. St Ives residents helped out by providing gifts of produce. The centre was also reliant on donations from well-wishers. Mrs Parker of Somersham gave a boiler and Mrs Powell a large mixing bowl. There were constant appeals for clothes for the evacuees who visited the centre.

In July 1943 the St Ives communal feeding centre was taken over by the newly established school meals service. When she left, after four years sterling service, Mrs Parker gave a party for seventy-six children at her own expense. The centre began to serve 140 meals a day to local children as well as evacuees. The meals were sent in from the school meals service central canteen at Over in Cambridgeshire.

Other communal feeding centres were set up, notably at the Trinity church social centre in Huntingdon. This was run by a Mrs Riley, who was an evacuee herself. The Mayor and Mayoress of Huntingdon, Mr and Mrs W.E. Driver, enjoyed 'an appetising and satisfying lunch, costing only 7d' on the first day. The Mayor commented that his lunch on the previous day 'at a hotel in the town where his son was stationed cost him over five times the price and it was not nearly so good.' The aim of the centre was to provide satisfying and economical meals for the evacuees and to ease the burden on householders. Centres were also needed in Ramsey, St Neots and Fletton. Godmanchester could manage because most of its evacuees were unaccompanied children. These communal centres soon began to open on Sundays because parents coming up from London to visit their children had nowhere else to go.

Just as it had been first with a communal dining centre, St Ives also led the way by setting up a communal laundry, the first of its kind in England. The laundry was set up in premises made available by Mr and Mrs F.M. Warren at The Priory and opened in September 1939. It was run by the WVS, with Mrs R.A. Savory in charge. Mothers of evacuees could go there and wash clothes. They were charged 6d for the use of the facilities. Even when many of the mothers returned to London, three London helpers and other volunteers continued the service, washing hundreds of garments each week. Unaccompanied children could have their garments washed for 2d per head (this was later increased to 3d). The laundry also offered a service for mending evacuees' clothes which proved a great boon for foster mothers. The laundry was to run for over five years. It was entirely self-supporting and was even able to make donations to various good causes from the profits.

More social centres were opened: at the Friends Meeting House in St Ives and at the Roman Catholic Room in East Street, St Neots. As the number of evacuees dropped by 1943, these rest rooms were open to members of the US Forces and the Women's Land Army.

Early in 1940, as evacuees began to drift back to London, fewer people were using these facilities. The communal kitchen in St Ives moved temporarily from the Corn Exchange to the smaller Co-operative Hall, but was still catering for more than sixty children a day.

LONDON'S SCHOOLCHILDREN

Finding space in local schools proved a problem. Evacuated schools were supposed to be kept together, so around 200 secondary school pupils were moved to Huntingdon, where the old grammar school was reopened. The girls from Highbury Hill moved into the old grammar school in May 1940. The sixth form art class painted a series of scenes along the corridor wall portraying the story of their evacuation, from leaving their school in London, to the countryside where they were billeted, the new grammar school and the old grammar school. The fifth space was left blank to show them returning to London.

Many Highbury Hill girls stayed for the entire duration of the war. In March 1942 Parnwell's Grocery Store, situated in the former Crown Inn in Huntingdon High Street, parts of which had not been used for fourteen years, was requisitioned and converted into a hostel for some of the Highbury Hill pupils. In November 1942, twenty-nine were able to move into the new hostel, which was run by a warden and cook-housekeeper. There were bunks for the younger girls, beds for the seniors, two bathrooms, a study room with settees and easy chairs. The headmistress welcomed the opening of the new hostel as an end to the 'billeting nightmare' in Huntingdon. The Highbury Hill girls became part of the community in Huntingdon, joining in with local activities, putting on concerts, making toys for hospitals and children's homes at Christmas and generally helping out with the war effort. When the school finally left Huntingdon on Friday 6 July 1945 they took with them many fond memories and left behind many friends. All the past and present foster patents were invited to an 'at home' party the week before they left. Several old girls also came up from London to say goodbye. Many of the pupils were invited back to Huntingdon for the holidays.

Around 100 boys from Woodland Park School, Tottenham, were transferred from Colne, Somersham, Pidley and Broughton to Godmanchester. Pupils from Tollington Park Central School, who had been at Somersham, also had to move. Almost 200 children and twenty-four teachers moved to Ramsey so they could attend Abbey Grammar School, but were eventually taught in the old grammar school and Methodist Schoolroom, so they only had to use the laboratories at the Abbey Grammar School. By the end of 1942, there were only about fifty evacuees remaining in Ramsey. Tollington Park Central School had been amalgamated with Highbury Hill School.

Buckden Towers was taken over as a secondary school for evacuees from Tollington Park Boys School. They sat at long trestle tables as there was not enough space for their normal double desks. The boys kept their books in card-

The children's sick bay in the schoolroom behind the Methodist church in St Ives, January 1940. (Norris Museum: PH/S.IVE/Waits/26)

board or wooden provision boxes. The Tollington Park boys were still at Buckden two and a half years later in March 1942.

In Eaton Socon, a large empty house on the Great North Road was used as a school. It had large gardens and up to 300 pupils could be accommodated. The hall at Hilton House, the home of S.J. Peters MP, was used as a school, as was the WI Hall in Ramsey.

In St Ives it was decided that local children would attend school from 8.30 a.m. until 12.30 p.m., and then boys from Finsbury Park and Highbury Vale would attend the same schools from 1.15 p.m. until 5.15 p.m. In the afternoons, the St Ives pupils would meet in various parts of the town for games or walks. The same arrangements were put in place in St Neots, Somersham and Spaldwick. In Ellington, parts of several gardens, including the Vicarage, were given over for evacuees to have gardening lessons. By 1940, the boys from Finsbury Park and Highbury Vale were having lessons at the Free church, using desks and apparatus sent up from London. Girls and infants from Highbury Vale used the Constitutional Hall in St Ives. Evacuees moved from place to place in an effort to have them educated full-time. A small school in Covington was reopened and, by January 1940, plans were in place to convert the WI huts in Warboys, Earith and possibly Bluntisham into schoolrooms.

Some schools were still split. There were thirty girls aged between three and nine, with three teachers and two helpers from Montern Street School, Tollington Park at Great Stukeley, fifty more at Little Stukeley, and others at Warboys. They were said to be settling in well, the *Hunts Post* commented that: 'from the wan faces induced by London life, they have developed ruddy complexions and already they have begun to put on weight.'

Things in general were so good in Huntingdonshire that the county was chosen to appear in a Ministry of Information film which would provide a record of the evacuation. Huntingdonshire was recommended due to the exceptional things being done by the WVS. Filmmakers visited the WVS stores at the old grammar school, the infants' nursery at Hinchingbrooke, the Trinity church schoolroom social centre and the St Ives communal laundry. They also filmed parents arriving from London to visit Huntingdon and St Ives, children in lessons and on a nature ramble in St Ives, a school in Warboys and a school changeover at Huntingdon Grammar School. The eighteen-minute film, entitled *These Children are Safe*, was shown in Huntingdon's Hippodrome in May 1940.

Evacuees began trickling back to London when things did not appear to be too bad there. By November 1939 a quarter of all the evacuees in St Ives had returned home. Several teachers had also left to reopen schools. The girls from Tollington High School left Great Gransden for Buckinghamshire and, after fourteen weeks in Kimbolton, 220 boys from Highbury County School left for Midsomer Norton in Somerset. However, forty-three pupils from Northfield School remained in Kimbolton for over three years. The Christmas holidays were kept deliberately short to prevent parents encouraging their children to return home. Despite this, the percentage of children returning to London was lower in Huntingdonshire than elsewhere.

Although many of the official evacuees had returned to London, plans were made early in 1940 for another 4,400 children to come to Huntingdonshire if London were to be bombed. It was envisaged that the billeting of these evacuees would be compulsory. People across the county protested that there was no more room due to the large number of unofficial evacuees who had arrived. Huntingdon's medical officer reported that the evacuees were 'upsetting the nervous condition of the female population of the town' who had to prepare breakfast, dinner and tea at two or three different times, due to the range of school times. In November 1941 the Huntingdonshire billeting officers resigned *en masse* as a protest against the use of compulsion. The job of the billeting officers was not an easy one, which makes it all the more remarkable that, in Huntingdon, the job was undertaken by Mrs Barbara Meadows. Aged just nineteen, Mrs Meadows was the youngest billeting officer in the country. On the instructions of the Ministry of Health, letters were sent out to householders across the county appealing for more billets. The response was very poor. The 1,554 letters sent out in Ramsey elicited only fifty-five replies, and 2,300 sent out in St Neots Rural District led to only 140 responses, and these offered only thirty new places.

As the fear of invasion increased after Dunkirk, infirm patients were evacuated to Huntingdon and St Neots from Public Assistance Institutions on the East Coast. Washingley Hall and Gransden Hall were requisitioned and equipped as hostels in case of a second evacuation. In June 1940, pupils from Hornsey High School came to Great Gransden Hall. Fifty girls were billeted at a hostel in the hall itself, which opened in December 1940. Others were billeted in Waresley, Abbotsley and the Gransdens. After a successful stay in the area, those from Hornsey left in August 1943 because numbers had fallen so much. By October 1940 there were 5,500 official evacuees in the county. The actual number was almost double that figure, with many unofficial evacuees also staying in the area.

Empty houses and cottages across the county were taken over to accommodate evacuee families. When the Blitz began, refugees who had lost their homes in London arrived in St Neots with nothing. A party of blind evacuees from Coventry was housed in the Swiss Cottage in Fenstanton. This party was looked after by Mrs Bennett, and remained in Fenstanton until March 1945. The Lamb public house in St Ives was also requisitioned and eight or nine mothers and children were housed there. In November 1940, the Manor House in Fenstanton, which was empty, was requisitioned as a communal billet for eight mothers, one grandmother and twenty-two children. Great Paxton Hill House accommodated children under two, cared for by Miss Robus. Children aged between two and five were housed at Riversfield in St Neots. Requisition continued for several years. In October 1943, for example, Huntingdon Borough Council requisitioned 3 The Walks North for a mother and seven children who had previously been billeted elsewhere. Sawtry Manor had been requisitioned in 1941. As time went on, even houses which had been condemned were being used to house evacuees. In 1941, six adults and ten children were living in a four-roomed house with no sanitation at Catworth.

The Particular Baptist Schoolroom in Crown Yard, St Ives was taken over as a clothes store. Clothes were always needed and the effort was aided by numerous gifts from America. Brampton Park was used as a clearing house for evacuees and it was full every night in October 1940. The Trinity church schoolroom, under the church, was known as the 'Refugees' Hotel'. It was open all day, solely for the use of evacuees and some 'deserving cases' were allowed to sleep there. Refugees arriving in Huntingdon were sent there and slept on mattresses on the floor. They would be interviewed by the billeting officer the following day. The number of evacuees in the county did not decrease over the next year or so. In May 1941 there were still 5,170 evacuated children in Huntingdonshire (the number of local school children was 7,975). These children had been sent by as many as seventy-four different authorities. By June 1942, however, the number had fallen to 2,566.

THE FINAL YEARS OF EVACUATION

As the war went on and the threat of bombing receded, the number of evacuees in Huntingdonshire fell. By June 1944 there were only fifty-nine Highbury girls left in Huntingdon and plans were made to merge with Huntingdon Grammar School from September. These plans had to be put on hold in August, however, once flying bombs again made London a dangerous place to be. This meant another influx of evacuees, mainly from the East End. On 7 July 1944, 200 evacuees arrived in Huntingdon and 140 in St Neots. The following day, St Ives received 139 more evacuees. A week later still more arrived: 113 to St Ives and 225 to the St Neots area but unfortunately their luggage went on to Huntingdon. Many unofficial evacuees swelled these numbers. Schools again became overloaded and half-day schooling was reintroduced in some places. The Free church schoolroom in St Ives was again called into action. A social centre for evacuee mothers was set up in St Mary's Hall in Huntingdon, the only town without one. As before, there was resistance from some to taking in evacuees and some local people were fined for refusing to accommodate the Londoners. Their number included a former Mayor of St Ives, Henry Stiles.

It was not until the summer of 1945 that the last of the evacuees left Huntingdonshire. Seventy children left St Ives on a special train, having been brought in from the villages by bus or WVS cars. Each one had a gift to take home with them. Just as when they arrived, the children left with coloured labels with their names and addresses attached to them. There were many tears and sad farewells.

CHAPTER 4

'On Standby': The RAF and Pathfinders

BEFORE THE WAR

Most of Huntingdonshire's airfields did not exist at the outbreak of the war. Indeed, the war was almost two years old before many of the bases were even begun. The airfield at Molesworth was only laid down in 1940, while the ones at Warboys, Little Staughton, Graveley, Kimbolton and Gransden Lodge were not built until the winter of 1941–42, well after the Battle of Britain had already been won.

In fact, in September 1939 the RAF only had two fully operational airfields in Huntingdonshire, namely Wyton, which had been taken over again by the RAF in 1937 after some years in private hands; and Upwood, laid out by the RAF in 1935 but not completed until two years later. Wyton had the privilege of being the home of Bomber Command's first operational sortie of the Second World War, when a Blenheim light bomber of No. 139 Squadron carried out a photographic reconnaissance flight over the north-west German coast on 3 September 1939. The bomber had been on standby since 1 September. One hour after war was declared it took off to see what the German fleet was doing. Crewed by Flt–Off. McPherson, Cdr Thompson and Cpl Arrowsmith, it took seventy-five photographs of the German fleet, which was later attacked.

The next airfield to be completed was Alconbury, which in 1938 had been just 150 acres of meadow. Even when Alconbury was finally declared operational (at the end of 1939) it was really just a collection of wooden huts. Bank clerk Philip Dickinson cycled past the new Alconbury site on Monday 4 September 1939, a day after war had been declared. He remembers: , 'I saw two Blenheim bombers land and there were a number of "fighters" there as well. All were camouflaged in a muddy brown and green colour. The great activity of the RAF everywhere was very noticeable – tenders and men rushing about everywhere.'

Most of the airfields in Huntingdonshire were in good locations. Gransden Lodge Airfield, home of a Canadian squadron for two years, had a secluded location which made it ideal for testing secret new equipment, such as the radio navigation system tested by Wellington bombers in 1942. Not everyone agreed

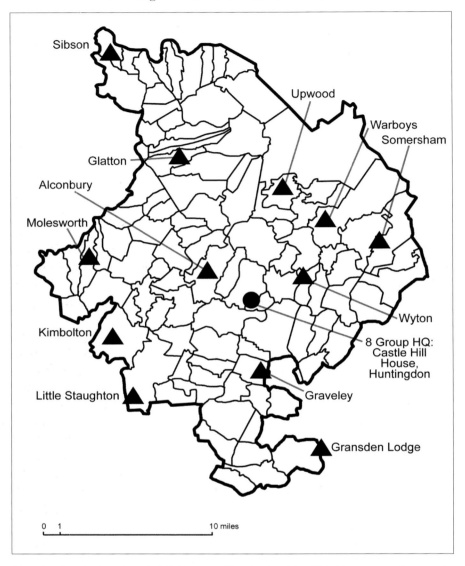

Map showing the location of airfields across Huntingdonshire. Airfields were usually named after the nearest town or village and often crossed parish or county boundaries. Graveley, Little Staughton and Gransden Lodge Airfields, although named after places outside Huntingdonshire, were partly or wholly within the county itself. (The authors)

that Huntingdonshire's airfields were in the right places. A plan to build a wholly new airbase for the Americans at Buckden came to nothing, following agricultural objections. The USAAF initially rejected RAF Kimbolton when they discovered that its runway was neither long enough nor safe enough for its B17s, though they did eventually return there after the runway was improved.

Huntingdonshire was busy with airfield construction traffic during the early years of the war. In 1941, dozens of lorries would collect sand and gravel from the railway station at Offord and then transport it along a narrow gravel track to Graveley where the airfield was being built.

Great efforts were made to disguise Huntingdonshire's airfields from the Luftwaffe. The most elaborate ruse was the construction of entire decoy airbases to lure the Germans into dropping their bombs on empty fields. Most RAF bases had satellite decoy airfields during the early years of the war. The basic 'Q'-style decoy was simply a lighting system which, at night, gave the impression from above of runways and hangars. A large field at Somersham was originally RAF Wyton's Q-style decoy, although from 1941 it was occasionally used to practise the deploying and collecting of secret agents in pitch black conditions. The more complex 'K'-style decoys actually had dummy aircraft and buildings and were intended to mislead daytime raiders. The Dutch barn at Bruce's Castle Farm, south of Conington, was bombed by the Germans as it had been disguised to look like a hangar from the air. The quality of the dummies was so good that in May 1942 someone even stole a dummy vehicle – 'a wooden truck, painted grey with rubber wheels' – from an RAF depot at Oldhurst.

At the same time, the real airbases were camouflaged so that they were less visible from the air. It seems unimaginable today that something as large as an airfield could be hidden, but the RAF did an excellent job. The metal roofs of sheds and hangars were painted to look like the tiling on domestic housing; many airfield roadways were laid out in curves rather than straight lines so that they looked like suburban roads and (most effective of all) the outlines of gardens and hedges were simply painted across runways in green paint. The RAF's airfields therefore seemed to melt into the existing hedging and field boundaries of the Huntingdonshire landscape. The success of these schemes was shown by the occasional failure of the RAF's own pilots to work out where their airfields were, resulting in aeroplanes making forced landings in meadows and fields. The Luftwaffe still found them however, during the early years of the war at least. The very first bombs to fall on Huntingdonshire soil fell on RAF Upwood and even the tiny airfield at Sibson, set up in July 1940 for pilot training, was bombed in August within weeks of its opening.

It is hard for people today to visualise the sheer size of these bases. RAF Wyton had accommodation for 2,293 men and 428 women (mainly WAAF), all housed in requisitioned buildings or Nissen huts. Molesworth, one of the largest, could accommodate 2,972 people by 1942, which made it roughly the same size as the whole of St Ives Municipal Borough (about 3,000 inhabitants in the 1940s). RAF Glatton also housed nearly 3,000 people. Local civilians had to pass through a guard post at RAF Glatton to enter nearby Conington.

At the height of the war, the eight airfields which belonged to Bomber Command's No.8 Group – Gransden Lodge, Graveley, Little Staughton, Upwood,

Tom Arnold, from Holywell-cum-Needingworth, served as a navigator with the RAF in No.138 and No.161 Squadrons. He is third from the right in this photograph, in front of a Lancaster bomber. (Nita Luxford)

Derelict aerodrome buildings on the site of Warboys Airfield today. (The authors)

Warboys and Wyton in Huntingdonshire, and nearby Bourn in Cambridgeshire – accommodated almost 17,000 people between them. This was a bigger population than any of Huntingdonshire's market towns at the time. The biggest town in Huntingdonshire during the 1940s, St Neots, only had about 7,000 inhabitants. RAF Bomber Command became the biggest single employer in the area. During the Second World War well over a quarter of Huntingdonshire's population worked for the Air Ministry.

THE PATHFINDERS

It is well known that Huntingdonshire was the base of the RAF's Pathfinder force, a force made up of expert navigators who flew ahead of the main bombing force to identify and mark out the targets, but it is not quite so well known why the RAF chose this area in the first place. In 1958 Pathfinder commanding officer, Don Bennett, recalled that, in 1942, he had been looking for an airfield which combined good communications, good transport links, and consistently above-average weather conditions:

> My selection, Wyton, as one of the best weather stations in England was fully justified. I managed to convince the Commander-in-Chief that I should have that station and also Oakington, both of which were 'permanent' built-up stations, and to these I should attach two satellites, Graveley and Warboys. Thus I started with four stations...'

In August 1942, Bennett established his headquarters at Wyton, where No.83 Squadron (flying Avro Lancasters) and No.109 Squadron (pressurised Vickers Wellingtons) were based. No.7 Squadron (Shorts Stirlings) went to Oakington (Cambs), No.35 Squadron (Handley Page Halifaxes) to Graveley and No.156 Squadron (unpressurised Wellingtons) to Warboys. The force therefore originally used a variety of different aircraft, but as it grew, and took in more and more airfields, it standardised on Lancasters and the new Mosquitoes. A permanent maintenance base was built at RAF Wyton for the Lancasters and another one at RAF Upwood for the Mosquitoes. Experts in navigation and bombing techniques worked out of a sprawl of Nissen and Lain wooden huts at Wyton Headquarters.

Bennett was a forward-thinking man. In 1942, Government scientists came up with a method to disperse fog at airfields, which they called FIDO – 'Fog, Intensive, Dispersal Of'. Other RAF group commanders laughed at the idea but Bennett saw its value and he organised a trial installation at RAF Graveley, the first of its kind in the country. The scientists set up 6,900 petrol burners along the main runway, essentially turning the airfield into an enormous Primus stove, burning superheated petrol to give a bright flame but little smoke. The first test

Castle Hill House in Huntingdon was the headquarters of the Pathfinder Force. Today the building acts as offices for Huntingdonshire District Council. (The authors)

The commemorative plaque at Castle Hill House. (The authors)

in January 1943 created so much flame that all the fire engines within 20 miles of Graveley rushed to the scene, but the Pathfinders stuck with the idea and in the long term FIDO undoubtedly saved lives. On 19 November 1943, for example, four Halifax bombers returning from raids over Germany discovered that their airfield was completely blanketed with fog, cutting visibility to less than 100 yards.

In normal circumstances the aeroplanes could easily have crashed as their pilots made desperate attempts to land without any idea of where they were, but the FIDO system was switched on, clearing a runway line which could be seen from 4 miles away.

There was some resentment over the loss of the aerodrome's rifle butts, which were used as targets for small arms firing practice. The butts consisted of an earth-filled brick structure about 25ft high, placed only 90 yards from the edge of the main runway and clearly a potential danger for damaged, difficult-to-control aircraft returning from missions. AVM Bennett wanted the butts removed, but the Works and Buildings group refused to do the work. The argument slowly worked its way up through the RAF hierarchy as far as the Air Ministry itself, which sent a team of bureaucrats from London to look at the place, but the aerodrome heard nothing more from the Ministry. In the end, Bennett gave up waiting for permission and blew up the rifle butts himself.

> An old 250lb bomb did all that was necessary... When the rubble was removed and the site was levelled and rolled, we had a good aerodrome again, and from my own personal knowledge I twice saw aircraft in trouble which passed exactly over the spot where that massive structure had stood. In both cases it would have meant the loss of all of those on board the aircraft concerned, one a Lancaster and one a Mosquito.

By the end of the war the Pathfinders were the largest single operational group in Bomber Command, controlling about 440 aircraft in nineteen squadrons, comprising eleven Mosquito and eight Lancaster squadrons. Between 18 August 1942 and 8 May 1945 the Pathfinders flew 50,490 bombing sorties and dealt with 3,440 targets. Some 3,618 airmen were killed out of a total Pathfinder force of about 35,000. This level of attrition, more than 10 per cent, was higher than Bomber Command's average for the war. Bennett's men used every flying trick in the book to evade the German anti-aircraft guns and to begin with losses were actually less than the Bomber Command average, which silenced the critics of the scheme. As the war progressed the Germans realised the danger that the Pathfinders represented and turned their full attention to destroying them. The Pathfinder response to this was to send decoy bombers alongside the main Pathfinders, which would divide the German defences.

The Germans realised that they could simply lure the main bomber force miles off course by lighting decoy Pathfinder flares in empty areas. The Pathfinders' counter-measure was to colour their flares. AVM Bennett wrote after the war:

> They were made in all colours and varieties, plain red, plain green, yellow, white, and each of those colours as a basic colour with ejecting stars of the same or

The wooden huts behind Castle Hill House in Huntingdon. (*Peterborough Citizen and Advertiser*)

One of the buildings built during the war in the grounds behind Castle Hill House still survives today. This building is now used by funeral directors William Peacock & Sons. (The authors)

The commemorative plaque at Gransden Lodge Airfield. (The authors)

different colours. Many combinations were therefore available for us to use as and when we chose, and the enemy could not copy them until he discovered what the colour of the night might be.

One of the most dangerous duties was to fly on the meteorological missions. Bomber Command had no way of knowing what the weather was like over occupied Europe, so fast unarmed Mosquitoes were sent out to discover conditions for the Pathfinders. No.1409 Meteorological Flight was based at RAF Wyton. All the weapons were stripped out of the aircraft to make them as light as possible, enabling the Mosquitoes to fly very quickly for long periods of time (some meteorological flights could last for almost twenty-four hours). Bennett wrote:

> They had no guns of any sort, and nothing offensive. I often wonder whether it was appreciated at Headquarters Bomber Command that they were asking an unarmed aircraft to proceed deep into the heart of enemy territory, often in broad daylight, without any cloud cover...There were some harrowing experiences for the crews of 1409 Flight when they were intercepted, particularly by the German jets just toward the end of the war, which could out-pace them but not out-manoeuvre them.

The most notorious mission was the controversial bombing raid on Dresden, on the night of 13 February 1945. Pathfinder aircraft led the way for a huge force of British and American bombers which created a firestorm. RAF Lancasters and Mosquitoes dropped 2,500 tons of bombs on the city in one night, killing an unknown number of people. Over the next two days B17 bombers from USAAF Molesworth also flew to Dresden as part of '1,000 bomber raids,' adding to the tragedy and chaos there.

Bomber Command also suffered many losses from its airbases in Huntingdonshire. Gransden Lodge lost 102 aircraft on operations during the war; Graveley lost 150; Little Staughton fifty-seven; Upwood sixty-six; Warboys ninety-nine; and Wyton, heaviest of all, lost 218. In total, more than 800 of Huntingdonshire's Bomber Command aircraft were destroyed on operations during the war.

CHAPTER 5

'Not Exceptionally Heroic': The County at War

After the first flurry of activity in many respects life in Huntingdonshire carried on much as usual. There were a record number of entries at the Huntingdon Steeplechases on Easter Monday 1940 and a crowd of 10,000 spectators attended. Indeed, the first excitement of the war itself only occurred in April 1940, when a barrage balloon, which had escaped from its moorings, had to be shot down by two aircraft over a Huntingdonshire village. It landed in a field belonging to Mr F.A. Cheney and was taken away by the military the next day.

This was soon followed by action of a more serious kind. Young naval recruits from Huntingdonshire took part in the battle at Norvik Fjord. Bernard Carter of Grafham, aged sixteen, and Roy Emmington of New Road in Ramsey, aged seventeen, were serving on the battleship HMS *Warspite*, while Sidney Cooper of Warboys, aged eighteen, was on HMS *Hostile*. At the end of April the *Hunts Post* reported the first Huntingdonshire casualty in action: Arthur James Flack, aged sixteen, from the Toll House in Earith and a former pupil of Colne Council School, was killed while serving aboard an anti-aircraft cruiser off Norway. He had been in the Navy since the age of fourteen.

A few weeks later, the reality of war came home to the people of Huntingdon town when two former grammar school pupils, Plt Offs Norman Smith (twenty-four) and Stanley Maddox (nineteen), were reported missing after air operations. A week later, at the end of May 1940, the first attack on British soil took place when a searchlight crew on the East Coast was fired on by enemy aircraft.

Many Huntingdonshire individuals signed up for military service, sometimes more than one from each family. Jack Metcalfe was living in Holywell-cum-Needingworth when he joined the Navy. He served throughout the war, on ships such as *Lady Kathleen*, *Ondina*, *Daldorch*, *Ranchi* and *Swift*. His brother, Bob, signed up for the RAF, as did his Holywell relative, Tom Arnold, who become a navigator with Nos 138 and 161 Squadrons, flying Lancaster bombers. His navigational notebook (including notes on navigation for the bombing of Turin and Arras) still survives today.

The increase in activity in early 1940 meant that the need for more air-raid shelters became urgent. In Ramsey, a temporary shelter was set up in the Old

The first fatality among Huntingdonshire men was sixteen-year-old Arthur James Flack, from Earith. Flack was serving with an anti-aircraft cruiser off the Norwegian coast when his ship was struck by a bomb. (*Hunts Post*)

Mill at the bottom of Great Whyte. In St Neots, which was not considered to be a target, it was felt that alleyways would give sufficient protection. St Neots Urban District Council was not happy about this and accused the county council of having 'an utter disregard for human life', but Lord Sandwich replied that shelters could not be built in case of a 'stray bomb'. St Ives asked for shelters, but there too the Ministry of Home Security recommended the use of narrow passageways as shelters for shoppers. The passageways had doors covered with zinc fitted and were labelled 'emergency refuge,' but these were often found to be jammed-up with bicycles. The people of Ramsey were also told to use passageways when the Old Mill shelter was declared structurally unsuitable.

At St Neots railway station, a basement in the goods office would accommodate up to fifty people, while in Huntingdon, one of the arches of the Brampton Road bridge was strengthened for use as a shelter for rail passengers. In Huntingdon the designated public shelters were not of much benefit. The one in the brewery needed duckboards to make it useable and was condemned in 1942 because it was damp and difficult to strengthen to requisite standards. Chivers Ltd in Huntingdon had dug out a shelter to accommodate its 300 workers and had its own air-raid siren. Huntingdon and St Ives air-raid sirens were at the police station. The Huntingdon siren was nicknamed 'Wailing Winnie'. By 1943, £22,000 had been spent on domestic air-raid shelters in the county: 5,782 individual domestic residences had been given brick surface shelters, 956 baffle protection and 6,116 had received Morrison table shelters.

By 1942 there were over 500 VADs working in hospitals, nursing homes, sick bays for evacuees, Paxton Park Maternity Home and ARP first-aid posts. Medical and surgical stores were placed in every village in case of invasion. There were three convalescent hospitals in the county, at Hinchingbrooke (used for air-raid casualties), Elton Hall and Conington Castle. The whole of the Swiss Cottage in Fenstanton was taken over for the care of the blind, while, at Holmewood Hall, Mr Fielden maintained blind patients at his own expense.

DUNKIRK AND THE FALL OF FRANCE

At the end of May 1940, King George VI asked everyone to pray for the safe deliverance of British forces in France. Almost immediately news from British soldiers serving abroad began to filter through to their families at home in Huntingdonshire. Local men serving in the Northants Regiment featured prominently in the battle at Oudenarde. 2nd Lt Anthony Brown, formerly of Whitwell House in Huntingdon, stated that: 'I cannot praise the Battalion enough. We were up against absolutely the whole force of the German attack, but our chaps behaved magnificently. It was the first time we had been machine-gunned from the air and it was not pleasant.'

Describing the embarkation of the British Expeditionary Force from Dunkirk, Lt Brown said 'it was absolute hell but our men never cracked up once.' 2nd Lt Brown lost everything while swimming to safety and arrived with only his battledress and a pair of sandals.

Two local men, Col. William E. Green and Capt. John H. Johnson, both from St Ives, were killed during the Dunkirk retreat. Col. Green, known to all as 'Weedy' was described as: 'A brilliant soldier, a daring leader and a Territorial commander of quite exceptional ability, the best type of English officer and gentleman... it is no exaggeration to say that he was idolised by every man in his battalion.' Col. Green had served in the Royal Flying Corps during the First World War. Before the war he had lived at Parkside in St Ives and worked as a dentist. Capt. Johnson, aged twenty-seven, had lived in Westwood Road in St Ives and had been a solicitor with Day & Sons Ltd.

Others were more fortunate. Sgt Geoffrey Hiscock of Avenue Road in St Neots was machine-gunned in Ypres and walked 10 miles with a bullet in his side. Clarence Ward, also of St Neots, was lucky to escape when a bullet pierced the top of his ear and his steel helmet.

Able Seaman Arthur Dobson, from Little Stukeley, formerly a porter at Huntingdon's LNER station, described the scenes at Dunkirk as 'a living hell.' His ship, *The Mosquito*, was bombed off Dunkirk and he was one of only two who escaped the ship without a scratch when the men were machine-gunned in the water. A French coin in his pocket saved him from a piece of shrapnel which would have 'gone straight through me,' he said. *The Mosquito* had made four trips loaded down with men before she was sunk. He arrived in England in just a singlet and a pair of shorts.

Earith bulwark showing the gun turret. (Cambridgeshire Libraries: Y.Ear.K7 1417)

RAF pilot John Peters, son of the local MP, Dr S.J. Peters of Hilton House, had been reported missing after being shot down over France. Although his parachute was riddled with bullets, he had survived after landing in a muddy field. After being helped on his way at a local farm, he had made it to Dunkirk in time for the evacuation. Within forty-eight hours he had been posted back on duty.

Forces personnel began arriving home on leave, or to their billets all over the county. A few were sent, exhausted, to the militia camp in Ramsey. They were dressed in tatters, some wearing legless trousers or armless jackets. A temporary camp was set up on the common in St Neots to accommodate weary soldiers arriving on the many buses. Eventually permanent wooden huts were built on the common and remained occupied until D-Day. They were given a hero's welcome. Soldiers returning to one village from Dunkirk were offered a meal despite it being the small hours of the morning. Women from the village also took the men's socks and while they slept, washed, dried and mended them. Their stories brought home to people that they were now in danger. Sirens sounded when aircraft passed over the county. The searchlights were on and distant explosions heard. There were air raids in neighbouring counties. The vicar of St Mary's church in Huntingdon announced that if an air raid occurred during a service, the hymn *Oh God our Help in Ages Past* would be sung, during which the ARP personnel would leave and others would move to the side and sit in the shelter of the walls. Col. and Mrs Wyatt arranged a first-aid post for animals injured in air raids at Hemingford Grey House.

Members of the Godmanchester (South Sector) ARP Service, photographed in May 1941. (*Hunts Post*)

After the capitulation of the French government, an anti-defeatist meeting was held in Huntingdon Market Square. Attitudes had changed. Those attending the race meeting at Newmarket were now condemned as 'heartless pleasure seekers', wasting petrol.

As more local men were called to join up, the *Hunts Post* featured a rousing editorial, talking of a county united against an enemy which was 'bent on our complete extermination'. Men were praised for answering the call to arms:

> It is not that we are exceptionally heroic... we know that the alternative to fighting would be infinitely more ghastly than the ruin which may result from the coming battle. Life without the liberty to which we are accustomed and shorn of those ancient rights and privileges which are the breath of life to the Anglo Saxon is just not worth contemplating.

The fear that people were feeling is shown by the fact that the editor had to remind them that defeat was not inevitable, as even Napoleon had failed to invade Britain.

There were very few conscientious objectors in the county. St Neots was proud of the fact that, although three COs had registered there, none of them were local men.

After the first year of war, seventeen men from Huntingdonshire had made 'the supreme sacrifice', twenty-nine had been wounded, fourteen were missing and fourteen were prisoners of war. The county had seen eight decorations for gallantry, including an OBE for Viscount Mandeville and the Military Cross for Capt. Desmond Barrie Goldie.

RATIONING AND CRIME

Despite all the preparations leading up to war, there were still shortages straight away. At the end of November 1939, Huntingdonshire's special constables needed mackintoshes, but none were available until March 1940. The provision of hot lunches at Huntingdon Grammar School had to be abandoned in November 1939 and the lunch break was cut to half an hour. Those not going home had to start bringing their own lunch to school. To conserve petrol, the afternoon post to Huntingdonshire villages was withdrawn in January 1940. The following month saw a serious coal shortage in Ramsey Heights, Ramsey St Mary's and Ramsey Forty Foot, forcing schools to close.

By January 1940, food rationing was on the cards. Concern was expressed in Huntingdonshire about the large amount of food being consumed by packs of hounds and by pigeons. In the meantime, hints and tips on conserving food were published in local newspapers and recipes were broadcast on the radio at 8.15 a.m. every morning. Regular cookery demonstrations were run by the 'Kitchen Front Club' at the B.C. & H. Electric Co. shops across the county. Local housewives were given recipe ideas and shown useful cookery techniques, such as making omelettes with dried egg and home-made tomato sauce.

> Those who have the will to win,
> Eat potatoes in their skin,
> Knowing that the sight of peelings,
> Deeply hurts Lord Woolton's feelings.

Soap rationing was introduced early in 1942. The day after its introduction, enterprising fundraisers at a dance auctioned a bar of soap in aid of Red Cross funds. It was sold many times over and raised £4 17s 6d.

Rationing often tempted people into crime. Small quantities of petrol were frequently stolen from military sources and drivers charged with using their vehicles for improper purposes. In 1942 Huntingdon was rocked by the discovery of a huge petrol conspiracy which touched many well-known members of the community, including the former high sheriff, Sir William Prescott. The scam had been going on for two years and involved falsification of documents and obtaining petrol without coupons. 'A long series of transactions dealing with enormous quantities of petrol in complete and absolute defiance of all the regulations' was how the *Hunts Post* described the affair. The three Murkett brothers, their manager and a garage owner from Godmanchester were at the centre of

VISIT TO M.O.F. KITCHENS

Huntingdon Recipes Taken To London

Mrs. W. E. Goodman, food leader for Huntingdon, recently accepted an invitation from the Ministry of Food to visit its headquarters in London and to view the various kitchens wherein all recipes are tested.

Mrs. Goodman, who lives in Priory Lane and is a member of the W.V.S., was the only food leader in the country to accept the invitation. She has had a lifetime's experience of cooking and in Huntingdon her job is to advise housewives on the best ways of using their rations to obtain well-balanced meals.

She took with her to London several recipes which the Ministry of food had not got but which were within the scope of wartime rations, and these she demonstrated to officials of the Ministry. The recipes were very favourably received, particularly those for apple shortcake and oatmeal pancake.

Our picture shows Mrs. Goodman at work on an egg and onion pie. During her visit she met the head of the Women's Institute in London and was also interviewed by representatives of the Press.

Mrs W. Goodman, Food Leader for Huntingdon, making egg-and-onion pie for the Kitchen Front Club, 1944. (*Hunts Post*)

the allegations. Nineteen people were fined a total of £5,020 for receiving petrol without coupons and seven were sent to prison.

Army and RAF camps were attractive targets for thieves. In 1941, army blankets and a battery were stolen from a camp in Hemingford Park, but the usual target was fuel. A quart of aviation spirit was taken from RAF Upwood on 2 March 1942, for example, and someone stole coal from RAF Molesworth on 7 April 1942. As the war progressed and more and more bombers were based in Huntingdonshire, huge amounts of fuel were being stored in the county's airfields. At least 45 gallons of petrol were stolen from jerry cans on a military lorry in St Ives on D-Day, 6 June 1944. A further 40 gallons of aviation spirit were taken from RAF Graveley on 27 February 1945.

Fuel was especially valuable during the cold winter of 1944/45. Even at USAAF Molesworth, coal for the stoves in the men's living quarters was being strictly rationed. The USAAF had to post guards on the coal dumps to prevent supplies being stolen during the night. Some men were so cold in January 1945 that they crept to the bomb dumps to steal the wax which was used to weather-proof the bombs, as the wax burned well.

More worryingly, ammunition was also frequently taken. In May 1942, twenty-seven rounds of .303 bullets were stolen from RAF Alconbury and a further 100 rounds of .22 bullets were taken from an army camp at Hemingford Abbots in November 1942. Less of a threat to the public, perhaps, was the theft of books. In November 1942, a member of the WAAF was arrested after she had lifted some volumes from the RAF library in Abbots Ripton Rectory. In August 1944 someone broke into a parked bomber at RAF Graveley, but all they stole was the clock from the cockpit.

An army batman stationed in Fenstanton sold army equipment to local residents. Mrs Elizabeth Fordham at The Bell had bought butter, tea, salmon, bacon, golden syrup and meat paste, while Mrs Edith Mansfield of The Crown and Pipes bought butter and tea. In October 1942, a member of the St Neots Home Guard was fined £5 for failing to hand in a German parachute he found. Obviously he was not the only one – lots of flares had been dropped by parachute, but very few 'chutes' had been found. The silk, one surmises, was used to eke out the clothing ration.

THE WVS AND THE RED CROSS

The Women's Voluntary Service was involved in almost every aspect of helping make peoples' lives easier. In addition to their work running services canteens and serving teas to passing troops and evacuees, the WVS also ran clothing exchanges to eke out the clothing ration. There was a clothing exchange at the social club in East Street in St Neots and another at the Friends Meeting House in St Ives. They staffed rest centres, ran the rural meals service and provided a volunteer car pool for ministry officials, hospitals and local government departments. The WVS was referred to as 'the army that Hitler forgot'. In 1941, the Huntingdonshire WVS had 2,000 members and even a 10hp Austin motor car, provided by Queen Marie of Yugoslavia, to help with their work.

Huge numbers of 'comforts for the troops' were being produced across the county. During four weeks in early 1940, for example, the WVS and other organisations produced 349 helmets, twelve cap comforters, 194 caps, thirty-five pullovers, five cardigans, 117 scarves, 349 pairs of gloves, 117 mittens and 315 pairs of socks, all of which were sent to the 5th (Hunts) Battalion of the Northamptonshire

Children of Broughton Church of England School, with the large blanket they knitted for Huntingdon Red Cross, 1940. (*Hunts Post*)

Regiment. Garments were also being provided for the anti-aircraft companies stationed in the county. Whist drives, dances and jumble sales were constantly being organised to raise money for wool. Women in Great Paxton were also knitting for the Paxton Park maternity home. The need for wool was so great that children were encouraged to gather wool from fences. This would be collected into 50lb sacks and sent to a central depot in Bradford. By 1943, Miss Flowers, one of the oldest members of the WVS in Huntingdonshire, had knitted 133 cardigans.

If the WVS weren't doing it, then the Red Cross were. They had a central depot in Huntingdon and fifty-seven work parties, running everything from Aid to Russia to comforts for the troops and POWs. The Red Cross frequently ran 'gift shops' selling home-made toys and such like. They raised considerable sums of money in this way, but their main service was running hospitals. The Hinchingbrooke House convalescent hospital had patients coming from sixty London hospitals. In 1944, 826 men (508 service personnel and 318 civilians), 733 women and three children were admitted to Hinchingbrooke.

The Red Cross nurses did an excellent job at Hinchingbrooke, according to Mr H.T. Baily of St Albans, who went there after being injured in an air raid on London in November 1940:

I can truthfully say I have never had better treatment in my life before. The staff were real Christians, always willing to help patients in whatever trouble they may have. The food was splendid and I shall never forget the four months I spent there.

Red Cross nurses being inspected on the Waits, St Ives, in 1940. (Norris Museum: PH/ S.IVE/Waits/38)

By the time it closed as a hospital in October 1945, 5,530 patients had been treated at Hinchingbrooke.

Elton Hall women's hospital had 120 beds; 1,055 patients were admitted during 1944. Conington Castle cared for fifty aged and infirm people, mainly those made homeless through enemy action. The Red Cross also maintained eight ambulances in Huntingdonshire

BUSINESSES AND THE WAR EFFORT

Great efforts were made by Huntingdonshire's businesses to contribute to the war effort. Murkett Brothers Motor Engineering Co. was busy overhauling, repairing and rebuilding vehicles for the Ministry of War Transport and Aircraft Production at the start of the war. Their 150 employees also converted private cars into ambulances. Over 1,000 vehicles were completely rebuilt for the services and many disused service vehicles were reconditioned. During the war the company carried out 44,987 repairs for the services. Many of these vehicles were used in the D-Day landings.

The Acoustical Manufacturing Co. transferred to Huntingdon in December 1940 when its London factory was damaged during the Blitz. Before the war they were making microphone and amplifying systems for theatres and hotels. The workforce turned to fitting loudspeakers to police cars, intended to help direct people to air-raid shelters, which were used all over the country. The company set up in Huntingdon using thirty-four untrained local girls, who worked double shifts. Some even had electric soldering equipment installed at home in order to keep the work going. Radio sets dropped by parachute from RAF planes to European Resistance organisations contained components made in Huntingdon. The Acoustical Manufacturing Co. had the main contract for radio coils and transformers for tank radio sets. At the peak of production they were making over 2,000 a week in Huntingdon. The company also researched and designed special components for use in motor torpedo boats.

With many British troops stationed abroad there was an urgent need to pack foodstuffs with the minimum of bulk to send to them. Chivers & Sons in Huntingdon had already been researching quick freezing, but turned their attention to the dehydration of vegetables. The success of their research meant that from the autumn of 1941 dehydration began at the Huntingdon factory. From February 1943 the plant was operating day and night drying and canning food. The employees were mostly women, working as fitters, sheet-metal workers and tractor drivers, jobs which had previously been considered 'men's work'. 200 local firms supplied food for processing, with any waste being sent back to the farms as cattle feed. Hundreds of thousands of canned peas, beans, spinach, celery, carrots, beetroot and potatoes were supplied to the British Red Cross for POW food parcels. The dehydration plant dealt with 10,000 tons of vegetables, mainly carrots, potatoes and cabbage for the forces. The production of powdered mashed potato was so successful that it continued after the end of the war.

Scotneys of London Road, St Ives had switched to war work fifteen months before the outbreak of hostilities. The company received an order for 20,000 bomb rack covers for dropping dummy parachute troops, to be made in three weeks. Not only that, the company also had to design a fitting for them. By working long hours and over the weekends, they fulfilled the order in a fortnight. Scotneys also made ladders for landing craft in Sicily and Italy, as well as for the National Fire Service. There was a dire shortage in London during the Blitz of 1942, at which time Scotneys were turning out between 5-10,000 a week, again having to work weekends to fulfil demand. The company also made hand-hose carts, platform and sack trucks, tent bottoms and Nissen huts. They assisted the Air Ministry in clearing aerodrome sites of timber.

Scotneys were also the only large firm catering for the agricultural industry, making tractors and trailers. Hundreds of car and lorry assemblies were being turned out each week, many of which played a part in the Libyan Desert campaign. When 8,000lb bombs were introduced, the firm's lorries had to be strengthened to carry them. Mr Tom Scotney himself, apart from being responsible for the troops' canteen in St Ives, did his best to aid the war effort. He was always willing to upgrade by scrapping old machinery as soon as new methods became available. Fifty men from the firm had joined the services. Luckily none were killed or wounded although the company accountant, Mr J. Bradshaw, spent most of the war in a Japanese POW camp.

Chivers & Sons Ltd, based in Huntingdon, supplied dried vegetables for the British forces and for Red Cross parcels sent to British POWs abroad. (Cambridgeshire Libraries: Y. Hun. K5 1614)

P. & H. Engineering in Hartford Road, Huntingdon, was set up by four businessmen, F. and A. Hand and B. and J. Paston, in September 1941 in response to a Government appeal. They carried out work for the Ministry of Aircraft Production making incendiary devices and embossed metal plates for photographic flashes. From 1942 onwards they were making metal liners for flare cases. Rows of boxes could be seen drying outside by passers by, although, of course they had no idea what they were to be used for. After Dunkirk, 200,000 of P. & H.'s incendiaries were dispatched against the enemy. 150,000 'flashes' were made for reconnaissance work. Many of P. & H.'s employees were evacuees or servicemen's wives, mainly working part-time, but were required to do overtime when necessary. Some cycled several miles from surrounding villages to work a twelve-hour day or a Sunday. At one time the workforce rose to over eighty, but there were never more than eight men, who included two Czech refugees.

Volunteer workers at Huntingdon Hosiery Mills assembled 40,000 gas masks when asked for help by the ARP before the outbreak of war. During the war the number of employees at the mill rose from 180 to 300. Socks from Huntingdon were on the march in every theatre of war. 6½-million pairs were supplied. In addition, between 1–2 million pullovers, jerseys and items of underwear were delivered to the forces.

Illustrations of an officer wearing a respirator, from the government's *Air Raid Precautions Handbook No.1.* (Cambridgeshire Libraries)

Silent Channel Co. Ltd in Huntingdon switched from the manufacture of window channels for peacetime motorists to reinforced hoses for use on army lorries to enable them to run in water. Up to 300 employees, 90 per cent of whom were women, also made oxygen breathing tubes for pilots which had to be able to cope with high altitudes. During the war years, over 2 million feet of hose were produced. The rubber mixing works was running day and night, six days a week making rubber for army tyres and rubber accessories for the army and ARP steel helmets. Due to the rubber shortage, the company was using up to 70 per cent reclaimed rubber. After the war the number of employees returned to the usual number of around sixty.

It was not only large manufacturing companies which did their bit for the war effort. Hunts Egg & Poultry Packers Ltd of St Ives were delivering eggs to London throughout the Blitz. Lorries had to enter the burning city, under instructions that deliveries must continue at all costs. Many of the workers were in the factory all day and carrying out ARP duties at night.

The Harrison family's basket-making and willow-growing firm in St Ives made airborne panniers to be dropped by parachute at Arnhem and collected by jeeps. They also made baskets for the navy, RAF laundry hampers and trolleys for the War Office. Several Italian POWs were employed by the firm.

Local building company F. B. Thackray & Co. were also involved in war work, building decoy aerodromes at Benwick and between St Ives and Somersham. In 1940 they were involved in the building of three anti-aircraft gun camps along the Thames Estuary. Camouflaged aircraft bomb stores at Lord's Bridge in Cambridge, American aircraft stores at Molesworth and buildings at Wyton and Westwood Aerodrome in Peterborough were among other projects completed by this Huntingdon company.

Local contributions were not all about combat. Paines & Co. of St Neots supplied beer to airfield messes and malt extract to both the services and civilians.

The London Brick Co. in Fletton saw new markets opening for its bricks in air-raid shelter construction. Substantial government contracts were made with London Brick from September 1939 onwards, especially for airfield construction, as millions of bricks were needed for bomb-proof control towers, accommodation, bomb dumps and other buildings. Production greatly increased but the distribution of all these bricks was severely hampered by government restrictions on road and rail transport. As the war progressed, the London Brick Co. built up such large stockpiles in its yards around Peterborough that some closed. The Somersham works was demolished and its bricks used for runway hardcore, while Warboys brickworks was closed in 1942 and its kilns were used to store high explosives, land mines, shells and torpedoes. Men working for the London Brick Co. had their hours reduced. By the end of the war, a record 500 million bricks were stacked at Fletton and its neighbouring yards.

CHAPTER 6

'Everything went Red': Bombing Huntingdonshire

After what seemed like months of agonised waiting, the Luftwaffe finally attacked Huntingdonshire on the night of 7 June 1940, when German bombers dropped fourteen high-explosive bombs on the RAF's airfield at Upwood. Two airmen were killed in the raid. Upwood villager Bill Bedford remembered the attack:

> About 2 a.m. an enemy aircraft followed one of our own into the landing area and dropped a salvo of bombs. To Laura and me it was just like the bombs dropping outside our home. We were so startled and frightened we both jumped out of bed and went underneath the stairs in a cupboard. About half an hour later the siren went off and being so ignorant of the warning and the all clear we both thought it was the all clear and went back to bed. At 4.30 when the siren blew the all clear, I jumped out of bed and said to Laura 'Come on the -------- are here again' and got back in the cupboard under the stairs. After this raid I decided to build an air-raid shelter.

RAF Upwood was targeted a further six times between June 1940 and August 1942, but there was little damage apart from bomb craters and some damage to an RAF Blenheim light bomber.

Wyton Aerodrome was bombed on 8 September 1940 and again on 10 April 1941. The Luftwaffe attacked Molesworth Aerodrome on 27 February 1942 and Kimbolton on 31 March. The airfields at Graveley, Gransden and Staughton were all attacked in August 1941. RAF Alconbury suffered the most. First bombed on 16 September 1940, Alconbury was bombed twice in one week in March 1941, and twice within forty-eight hours in June of that year. Alconbury's airfield had been hit by a total of forty-six high-explosive bombs by the end of August 1941, more than any other airfield in the county. Amazingly there were no casualties from any of these attacks.

In January 1941, there was great excitement when a German bomber swooped down over Huntingdonshire, bombing the army camp on St Neots Common. Home Guard snipers fired at the plane, which machine-gunned a lorry (fortunately, it was empty), leaving seventy bullet holes in it. Houses, gardens and a

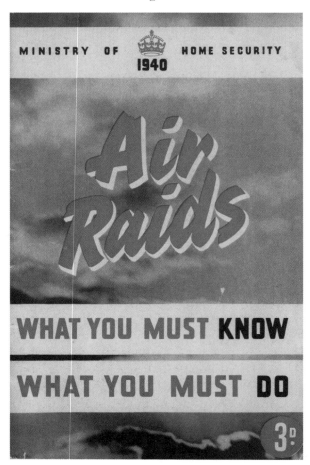

MINISTRY OF   HOME SECURITY
1940

Air Raids

WHAT YOU MUST KNOW

WHAT YOU MUST DO

3D

The government brought out much advice and publicity in 1940, telling the public what they should do in the event of an attack. (Cambridgeshire Libraries)

nearby gravel pit were also shot at. Many people, including children, came out of their houses to look, but the German did not fire at them. The *Hunts Post* reported a second raid on a 'home counties village'(Godmanchester) two months later. A single German plane dropped flares and incendiaries and machine-gun fire was heard. Mr Gadsby's farm and Mrs Randell's house were damaged and telephone wires were brought down. One stick of bombs fell on some allotments and 'messed up' some cabbages. Pheasant feathers were found by one of the bomb craters, so there was at least one victim. At least eighteen incendiaries fell near haystacks, but none were set alight.

Incendiaries were such a threat that fire-watching procedures had to be put in place. In the villages volunteers were generally forthcoming to maintain a twenty-four-hour fire watch. At Huntingdon Grammar School the watch was carried out by teachers and older pupils. Fire-watching posts were set up in Huntingdon, one at the Town Hall and one at the Blind Society shop – the latter 'manned' entirely by women. Buckets of water, stirrup pumps and other anti-fire equipment were to be kept near the doors of business premises. Demonstrations of how to extinguish fires caused by incendiary bombs using a stirrup pump were held all over the county. Huntingdon's fire watch soon numbered 164 people. The two main posts were supplemented by nine posts in residential areas. In addition there were sixty privately owned stirrup pumps in the borough. Ramsey's fire-watching post was in the Sports Hut.

Many bombs fell in the villages and farms around the RAF airfields. Huntingdonshire County Council's ARP officers counted that at least 340 known bombs had fallen on the county up to end of 1940, but the towns were largely safe. Then the Germans changed their tactics to concentrate on bombing urban areas rather than airfields. With the exception of two bombs dropped on Hinchingbrooke back in March, Huntingdon had so far escaped the bombing, but on the night of 12 August 1941, the Luftwaffe dropped at least forty-seven high-explosive devices on the town, forty-four of which exploded. (A further nine bombs were dropped on Warboys the same night.)

Ramsey was bombed on 22 August 1942, at about 11.10 p.m. A lone German aircraft circled the town two or three times before dropping at least five high-explosive devices, four of which exploded on impact. Two bombs detonated within 50 yards of the main telephone exchange, knocking it out, which meant that the town's response system failed to act for the first fifteen minutes. Fortunately, both the ambulance depot and rescue party headquarters leaders acted on their own initiative when they realised that telephone communications were impossible. Only a few people were in the town centre when the bombs fell, but seven people were killed and several more injured, including two elderly evacuees, making it the worst single bombing incident in Huntingdonshire in the entire war. Hector Campbell and Wilfred Tatt took shelter in a passage and were buried beneath masonry when a bomb fell directly above them. Twenty homes were demolished and thirty more badly damaged and residents had to be evacuated. The roof of the council school was taken off and the windows of the Methodist chapel blown in. The schoolroom which had been designated as a rest centre was unusable. The stock of blankets and mattresses was buried beneath the debris. Locals believed that the bomber had been attracted by the lights from several buses which were in the area at the time. The St Ives ARP rescue party was sent to help out the locals. Mr G. Richardson, Ramsey's own man in charge, was commended for his excellent work, even though his own house had been wrecked.

On Friday 4 September 1942 bombs were dropped on Yaxley. Young Elizabeth Blackman was at home that evening with her brother Peter, her mother Marjorie, her grandparents Arthur and Kate Sharpe and her Aunt Lily. She remembers:

A lone plane flew overhead and seemed to circle around. My grandmother said 'That is a German plane, it does not sound a bit like one of ours.' My mother

The results of an air raid at
Fletton on 16 November 1940;
six high-explosive bombs fell
over Queens Walk, Orchard
Street, London Road and
Park Street, damaging thirty-
one houses and demolishing
two. (County Record Office
Huntingdon: 4440)

answered quickly, 'Stop worrying so, Mum, you have got German bombers on your mind.' With that they heard a whistle followed by an explosion. The foundations of the house heaved. The paraffin lamps shook and flickered and every bell in the hall rang. My grandmother ran up the back stairs with a candle to my grandfather who was already out of bed but having trouble finding his trousers! My mother ran up the front stairs to fetch my brother. All safely back downstairs in the kitchen there seemed an awful silence...

Next morning it was discovered that the house was surrounded by unexploded bombs, and the army arrived to defuse them. More bombs were discovered in a field close to Yaxley crossroads, another cluster fell on the poultry houses at the back of the Co-op farm, another on Yaxley Lodge Farm and some more near the railway.

A few bombs fell at St Neots, but it is believed that these had simply been jet-tisoned by a Luftwaffe bomber returning from a mission elsewhere, rather than a raid on St Neots in its own right. High-explosive bombs fell onto a field north of Mill Lane, followed by a further seven incendiaries which fell on farmland, today part of the Longsands estate, just east of Avenue Road. Wardens Bill Key and Jim Griffin saw incendiary bombs land on waste ground just north of Albert Terrace in Cambridge Street. The whole area was lit up by the incendiary explosions as brightly as daylight.

Bomb damage at Fletton, November 1940. (County Record Office Huntingdon: 4440)

The power station at Little Barford, however, just across the river from St Neots, was a popular target for German bombers. St Neots resident Eric Davies saw one such attack take place during the middle of an afternoon:

> As I was crossing the open space between the St Neots road and the Power Station I heard a plane approaching behind me from the east, and looking around, from the twin tails of the aircraft I first thought it was a British Hampden bomber, but the black crosses soon identified it as a German Dornier bomber flying low across the site. I watched with others as the aircraft flew over the building, turned and returned to the road, where it was obviously preparing for another probably attacking run... One bomb exploded on a concrete road in front of the building and from my cement 'shelter' I have a vivid recollection of a drum of wire-armoured cable rising about 20ft into the air, where a side came off, projecting a long spring-like spiral of cable sideways before falling to the ground completely ruined.

Shrapnel from the bombs cut the cooling tubes to three of the huge transformers at the power station, so Davies and his colleague, Jimmy Linford, ran across the site to turn off the transformers before they overheated and exploded, dodging German bullets as they did so:

Another view of
the damage done at
Fletton, November
1940. (County
Record Office
Huntingdon: 4440)

After it had obviously dropped all its bombs the aircraft made three runs, machine-gunning in all directions, and it was fortunate there were no casualties... I could hear bullets hitting the side bags and could clearly see the enemy gunner in the front turret of the aircraft as it passed over.

The Luftwaffe later made more attempts to destroy the power station during night-time raids, and work on building new generators was delayed as bombers had destroyed much of the necessary equipment.

On another occasion a single bomb was dropped on Abbotsley, scoring a direct hit on an air-raid shelter in a council house garden. The family only survived because they had not bothered to enter the shelter when they heard the siren. According to C.F. Tebbutt, the owner of the house was more concerned that the blast had released his ferrets, which then killed his chickens, than about the danger to his family.

Some destruction was caused by the RAF successfully shooting down German aircraft. At 2 a.m. on Sunday 5 October 1940, a German Junkers bomber was shot down by fighters near St Neots. It crashed into a field and exploded. The *Hunts Post* reported that 'parts of the machine and fragments of uniform were found 300 yards away. Buildings a mile off were shaken, windows rattled and flames were seen nearly 10 miles from the spot.' There were no survivors. The only casualty on the ground was a pheasant.

Three RAF Hurricane fighter planes gave chase to a German Dornier bomber across Huntingdonshire on 24 October 1940 and shot it down in Bell Farm Fields at St Neots. A large market day crowd ran for cover as the bomber swooped down towards the town, but most could not resist watching what happened. One eye witness said 'The speed of the RAF planes... made the Dornier look like a farm wagon against a modern sports car.' Three crew died, while a fourth, who parachuted into Bushmead Road, was critically injured and arrested. The RAF pilot did a victory roll over St Neots before flying off. The Dornier 215 was one of the Nazis' newest aircraft and this was the first of its kind to be shot down over Britain. Workers at Little Barford power station watched the whole spectacle and (as it was a Friday, and payday) gave generously to the Spitfire Fund appeal. Unfortunately, a local policeman died when he was electrocuted trying to douse a hedge fire which had been started by electrical power lines brought down in the crash. A few weeks later, a ring made from the windscreen of the Dornier was raffled by Eaton Socon WI at their 'American Tea'.

ARP EXERCISES

Although the Germans never, in practice, dropped gas bombs on Britain, it was still a possibility and major exercises were carried out to simulate gas attacks. The purpose of the exercises was to ensure that everyone knew what they had to do in the event of a real gas attack. They had to be as realistic as the ARP could make them, which meant using real gas. In 1942, therefore, Huntingdonshire's Civil Defence Committee purchased 150 tear-gas generators, which they then proceeded to use in many of Huntingdonshire's towns.

The first town to be gassed in this way was Ramsey. At 6.00 p.m. on 28 February, thirty generators, located next to the Wesleyan Methodist chapel on the High Street, were used to generate tear gas. The purpose was to make people use their gas masks. The concentration of gas would demonstrate that it was no good just to run inside. The resulting gas cloud was most impressive. 'The effect of the gas was felt beyond the clock on the Great Whyte, and for 70 yards on the East and 50 yards on the West of the point of release,' wrote the assessor in his report. On 25 April 1942 another thirty generators were used to gas St Neots. The tear gas was released in Cambridge Street, just east of the traffic lights, at 6.30 p.m. The air-raid wardens practised their alarm-raising and first aid on casualties, while the police controlled the traffic. On 2 May tear gas was let off in Crown Street in St Ives, alongside some Thunderflash bombs, in order to simulate genuine explosions.

Huntingdon's exercise was held at 6.00 p.m. on 8 April 1942, when twenty-five gas generators and two Thunderflash smoke bombs were detonated in the High Street opposite W.H. Smiths. The tear-gas cloud lingered for almost half an hour and was strengthened by the firing of a further ten gas generators. Four people

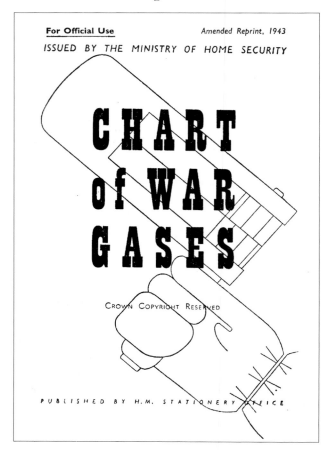

For Official Use   Amended Reprint, 1943

ISSUED BY THE MINISTRY OF HOME SECURITY

CHART
of WAR
GASES

Crown Copyright Reserved

PUBLISHED BY H.M. STATIONERY OFFICE

In 1943 the Ministry of Home Security issued this booklet, giving advice about the different types of gas which could be expected in an attack. (Cambridgeshire Libraries)

had to be taken to hospital. 'The smell and effect of the tear gas was felt inside the Post [Office] almost immediately after release,' wrote the umpire in his report. 'More practice is required by the nurses in the irrigating of eyes, as none except the Sister-in-Charge appeared to be very skilful.' Even the Thunderflash smoke bombs were a problem as they almost caused a road traffic accident in the centre of town. A small crowd of people, mostly children, gathered in Huntingdon to see the gas let off. Quite a few locals were caught without their gas masks. The gas test in St Ives in May 1942 revealed that many gas masks were faulty.

The tear-gas exercises were intended to simulate just one form of gas, 'non-persistent' gas, which tended to disperse quickly. Huntingdonshire's Civil Defence planners were well aware that the Germans could easily use 'persistent' gas, such as mustard gas, generated by a chemical reaction in a pool on the ground and which would last for as long as the pool of liquid was there, possibly many hours. Real mustard gas was far too dangerous to use in an exercise but alternatives were available. In Huntingdonshire the ARP wardens created a solution of two chemicals – three parts 'G2D' to one part 'Z' – which they laid down in a pool on the ground. Unfortunately, the resultant gas was not very impressive visually and during Fletton's blister gas exercise on 3 May 1942, for example, spectators wandered through the cloud of gas unharmed and highly amused. The Huntingdon exercise assessor suggested mixing the chemicals with soot 'to produce an appearance more like mustard, rather than mere dampness.'

One ARP exercise in November 1942 was made more realistic when fires and an 'incident' involving a high-explosive bomb was arranged by Mr Shearcroft, science master at King's School, Peterborough, and Mr Stewart, chemistry master at Huntingdon Grammar School. Both had attended a special gas course.

SAVING THE HERITAGE

One of the more interesting civil defence jobs was to draw up a list of the county's historic buildings, those which it was believed might be worth saving if hit by a German bomb. Architects Sidney Inskip Ladds and William A. Lea drew up a preliminary list in July 1941. It was made up mainly of parish churches (perhaps unsurprisingly as Ladds was Diocesan architect), but it also included the Manor House in Hemingford Grey, which was (and remains today) England's oldest continually inhabited domestic building; the old grammar school where Oliver Cromwell and Samuel Pepys had been taught and Cowper House in Huntingdon. Their list also included the three medieval bridges in Huntingdon, St Neots and St Ives, which had been earmarked for destruction by the British themselves if the Germans really did invade and also Cromwell's Barn in St Ives, which ironically would be demolished in the 1960s anyway.

What is perhaps more revealing is the group of buildings which were not on the list. Godmanchester, for example, boasts a variety of historic buildings but interestingly only two, the parish church and Corpus Christi House, were thought to be worth saving. 'A few of the buildings are good,' according to handwritten notes on one surviving copy of Ladds and Lea's list, 'but many are mean in the extreme.' Orton Longueville Hall 'seems very bad and not worth preserving.' The maze at Hilton was regarded as 'a mere obelisk, [it] will be destroyed or will escape.' Their comment on Fenstanton's clock tower was that 'we really do not think it is worth putting on the list, but we raise no objection if you wish it to be included'. The clock tower was indeed added to the list a few months later, following local protests.

One unforeseen consequence of the war was the rescue of Huntingdonshire's written heritage. In March 1941, Air-Raid Warden Philip Dickinson was in an underground store under Huntingdon's Market Square looking for old documents for an exhibition for 'War Weapons Week' when he discovered an old iron safe, so old that its lock and hinges had rusted up. Using a pair of tongs he forced

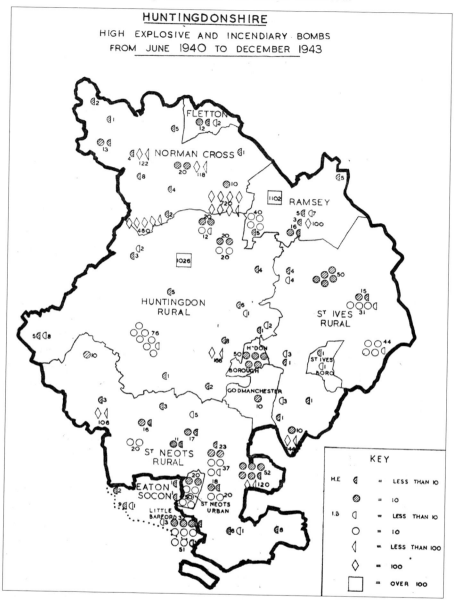

Map showing the areas where bombs fell in Huntingdonshire, up to December 1943. Taken from *Air Raid and Other War Incidents in Huntingdonshire*, 1944. (County Record Office Huntingdon)

it open. Inside the safe were fourteen of the earliest charters for Huntingdon, including the original charter of King John from 1205, the charter of King Charles from 1630 and the foundation charter of Huntingdon Grammar School. No one else had seen these records since the nineteenth century.

ALLIED CRASHES

From 1942 onwards the main danger came not from Luftwaffe bombs but from crashing Allied bombers. Air-raid documents kept by Huntingdonshire County Council show that there were at least eleven major crashes during the two-year period from March 1943 to April 1945, either from damaged aeroplanes limping back to base after a raid or, far more dangerously, aircraft loaded with bombs exploding on take-off.

One such crash happened at 9.19 p.m. on the night of 4 March 1943, when Lancaster bomber No. W4333 hit the ground near Yaxley, soon after taking-off. Yugoslav pilot Mebosja Kujunzie ordered the rest of his crew to bail out while he guided the plane away from the village, thereby averting a greater tragedy at the cost of his own life. Two other crewmen were injured, two were uninjured and the bodies of the remaining three simply could not be found. The plane itself was burnt out.

Clive Dellino, an evacuee from London, was living in Yaxley at the time:

If they [the bombers] were too damaged to land, the pilots would try to get near to their home airfield so that the crew could use their parachutes, set the aircraft to fly by itself and jump out at the last minute before it crashed to the ground. Sometimes a very brave pilot would choose to fly his plane until it hit the ground, to steer it clear of houses and people. This was what happened when one fell near us, in open fields. It is quite possible that I am still alive today because that pilot died avoiding our school.

Two months later another British bomber failed to make the runway on its way back from a mission and crashed at Toseland, damaging a barn and some telephone wires in the process.

An American Mustang fighter also crashed near Yaxley, on 27 September 1944. The wreckage lay buried in the fens until September 1990 when it was located and excavated. The fighter had crashed in Mrs Barnes's garden. She escaped death by yards and was later asked by C.F. Tebbutt if all crew had been killed. 'Oh yes, and all my rabbits as well,' she replied. People had become quite blasé about death.

The worst incident happened on Monday 5 October 1942, when a Wellington bomber from No. 156 Pathfinder Squadron at Warboys crashed at Somersham, killing ten civilians, ranging in age from Pauline Catterick who was just eleven months, to Annie Mary Holdich, aged seventy-four. Another of the dead was a sixty-seven-year-old evacuee from Norwich. At least six others were severely injured. Seven houses were wrecked by the crash or gutted by the huge fire which followed. The plane, which had just taken off, was loaded with fuel which added to the conflagration. It was about 7.15 p.m. when the plane came down in West End, smashing into cottages adjoining the White Lion pub, several of which were thatched. The aircraft took off the roof of a house in Rectory Lane. Mr and Mrs

Len Ruff, who were downstairs at the time, miraculously escaped injury. It went clean through the cottages next to the White Lion and came to rest in the cottages on the opposite side of the street.

Firemen, members of the Home Guard, civil defence workers, soldiers and airmen all fought heroically to put out the blaze. They were joined by firemen from St Ives and Huntingdon. The St Ives rescue party was first on the scene. They later had the aid of the county 'heavy rescue party'. The men from St Ives were relieved the next day by rescue parties from Ramsey and Huntingdon. Mobile canteens from Huntingdon and Chatteris served hot drinks, soup and sandwiches throughout the night. The crew who had bailed out landed safely on the Bluntisham to Oldhurst road, unhurt apart from a twisted ankle. They had been forced to abandon the aircraft when a flare ignited and caught fire.

By the time the dead were laid to rest, the crash had claimed an eleventh victim. Four-year-old Juliana Davies died in hospital on Wednesday. The child's mother had severe burns and her grandmother, Mrs Eliza Nightingale, was dead. The other victims were Mrs Violet Maule, her daughter Mrs Vera Catterick and her granddaughter Pauline Catterick; Mrs Alice Lamb and her son Frank Lamb; Mrs Annie Holditch and her daughter Mrs Elsie Taylor; Mrs Elizabeth Richardson and Ena Stroud, aged fifteen. Among the mourners at the funeral were the Earl and Countess of Sandwich, Dr S.J. Peters MP, and other dignitaries. Members of the crew of the ill-fated aircraft were also in attendance. An RAF lorry covered in flowers carried all eleven victims through the streets of Somersham which were lined by the entire population of the village. An RAF plane circled overhead and dipped one wing in salute. Sir Arthur 'Bomber' Harris himself visited the aerodrome on 9 October to give the crews encouragement after this tragic incident.

On the night of Saturday 6 November 1943, two Wellington bombers, taking part in a night flying exercise, collided over Huntingdon. One came down near Abbots Ripton, the second just yards from the Officers' Mess at Brampton Park. Capt. Clay Snedegar, an intelligence officer based at Brampton Grange, was first on the scene at Brampton:

> There was a terrific explosion, sending flames 100-150ft high. Machine gun ammunition was exploding in all directions from the heat. It was dark and the billowing flames lit up the sky like daylight… One of the bodies pulled from the wreckage was that of a young woman. She was a brown-haired girl and the flames from the wreckage lit up the golden tones in her hair… For nearly a 100 yards in all directions, bits of plane, grass and trees were burning fiercely… At the base of a very large tree was the body of the fifth crew member. He was lying face down with his head jammed against the base of the tree… The impact had knocked off his flying boots: they were 2 or 3ft from his body.

Only the pilots from each plane survived.

RANK	SHOULDER MARKINGS (BOTH SHOULDERS)	STEEL HELMET
Chief Regional Fire Officer		
Fire Force Commander		
Assistant Fire Force Commander		
Divisional Officer		
Column Officer		
Senior Company Officer		
Company Officer		
Section Leader		
Leading Fireman		
Fireman		

Right: Sketch showing the shoulder and steel-helmet markings of members of the National Fire Service. Taken from *The Advanced Auxiliary Fireman*, 1942. (Cambridgeshire Libraries)

Below: An RAF lorry bears the bodies of the eleven victims of the Somersham air crash to their last resting place. The streets were lined with members of the Home Guard and other soldiers. Airmen acted as coffin bearers. (*Hunts Post*)

Less than three weeks later, another tragedy occurred at about 4.54 p.m. on the afternoon of Friday 26 November 1943, when a Pathfinder bomber, fully laden with bombs, sitting at RAF Wyton's dispersal point near Ramsey Road and waiting for its turn to take-off on a mission to Berlin, simply exploded for no ascertainable reason. Five RAF men and one civilian were killed in the blast. Mechanic Marcus George Cook, a forty-two-year-old father of two and a former RAF man, was passing the aerodrome on his bicycle when the plane exploded, flinging him from his machine and killing him instantly. The explosion overturned a butcher's van standing nearby: Herbert Skinner, the driver of the van, was seriously injured and died in hospital four days later. Twelve adults and six children had to be evacuated from the nearby cottages after slates were torn off roofs, windows blown out and internal walls demolished. Only the fact that they happened to be at the rear of their cottages saved the residents from serious injury.

Seven houses were made uninhabitable by the blast. Mrs Silk, who was made homeless in the explosion, said:

> The whole house seemed to fall around me. Everything went red, and then black. The kitchen table shot across the floor and glass flew everywhere. I had just gone to the back door to pay for some sweets my little daughter Eileen aged seven was buying, otherwise I must have been injured.

The explosion broke windows in St Ives, 8 miles away and caused damage as far away as Willingham.

Just eight weeks later, on 25 January 1944, another Lancaster from the Pathfinder force crashed in the village of Upwood, killing its crew and destroying a house. This was the second time Upwood village had been hit, as a similar incident occurred in August 1941, when the thatched roof of Carlton House caught fire. 'I think it [the bomber] didn't really get going and it crashed,' one villager remembered. 'The fuselage part of it went on our roof, and caught on fire... it was quite frightening.'

On 18 November 1944, Lancaster No.PB197 from Graveley Aerodrome crashed on Weald Farm in Huntingdonshire, about 1 mile west of Croxton, killing five of its crew. Ray Meeks, a lifelong resident of Toseland, recalled that 'as a young boy I remember this particular aircraft returning on what was a foggy night. It was flying really low – just clearing the hedges. Then it lost height and crashed.' Parts of the bomber are now at the Pathfinder Museum.

Eight crewmen died when Lancaster No.PB669 from RAF Warboys crashed and caught fire near Spaldwick at about 1.10 p.m. on 11 March 1945, just a few weeks before the German surrender.

The Americans in Huntingdonshire had disasters, too. On the evening of 27 May 1943 a B17 Flying Fortress bomber, No.42-29685 of 412 Squadron

Lancaster bomber R5868 at the RAF Museum, Hendon. This bomber, the oldest surviving Lancaster in the world, flew for a few months as a Pathfinder aircraft with No.83 squadron, based at RAF Wyton. (The authors)

of the 95th Bomb Group, exploded on the ground at Alconbury while it was being loaded in preparation for a mission. A single 500lb bomb detonated for an unknown reason, setting off all the neighbouring bombs, destroying the B17, killing eighteen men and injuring another twenty-one. A further three B17s were completely destroyed in the blast and eleven more were damaged.

On 14 October in the same year a damaged B17 bomber, nicknamed *Bam Bam*, was trying to return to Molesworth, but the airbase was hidden in fog and the pilot, with the aircraft low on fuel, ordered his crew to bail out: the B17 flew on by itself for about 10 miles before crashing into a house in Riseley, Befordshire. An explosion on board a B17 soon after it had left Molesworth Airfield, on 10 June 1944, blew the tail off the aeroplane and sent it crashing into the ground a quarter of a mile west of Great Gidding. On 23 January 1945 another B17 bomber crashed while taking-off from Kimbolton Airfield in bad visibility, ploughing into the accommodation areas. Four crewmen managed to bail out, but another six died in the crash.

On 5 April 1945 the B17 *Miss Ida* caught fire after take-off from Glatton. The pilot tried to return to base but crashed into a haystack, creating a hole 5ft deep and 30ft wide in the ploughed field. One crewman was thrown clear and survived.

A statue of USAAF
Cdr James Doolittle,
at the Imperial War
Museum, Duxford.
(The authors)

A particular danger was the possibility of mid-air collisions. American pro-
cedure was for a squadron's bombers to form into a group immediately after
take-off, a practice known as 'assembly'. Bombers would continually circle their
airfield until all the planes had taken-off, whereupon they would head towards
Germany in formation. By 1943, assembly involved so many large and unmane-
ouverable aircraft that collisions became frequent.

Not all crashes led to disaster. At midday on 19 February 1944 a Lancaster
from RAF Wyton crash-landed at Hinchingbrooke, near the farm, but there were
no bombs on board, the aeroplane did not catch fire and no one was injured.
On 28 April 1945 a Lancaster from RAF Warboys crashed at Brampton, slightly
injuring two of its crew, but despite catching fire there was no further damage.
One Mosquito aeroplane which crashed on 6 June 1944, on its way to bomb
German defences in Normandy as part of D-Day, had a 4,000lb bomb on board
which failed to go off. Nearby houses were evacuated and the bomb was successfully defused. Another lucky moment occurred on 24 February 1943, when two
bomb-laden B17s collided in mid-air over Molesworth. One B17 smashed off the
rudder of the aeroplane beneath it, but fortunately both aircraft landed safely and
there were no injuries.

Another lucky escape was that of US Cdr James Doolittle (the creator of the
famous 'Doolittle Raid' on Tokyo), who was visiting Kimbolton on 6 March
1944. He was almost killed when a returning B17 lost control on landing and
hurtled past the control tower in which he was standing. Doolittle missed death
literally by inches.

The RAF once even managed to bomb their American colleagues. On 6 July 1944 the B17s of USAAF Molesworth were practising night flying, which meant that Molesworth was lit up with hundreds of runway and approach lights. A single RAF bomber assumed it was the local bombing training range and dropped two bombs. The first went through the roof of a hangar, while the second narrowly missed the control tower.

Allied bombs were usually kept in specialised bomb dumps on the edges of airfields, well away from civilian residents and the base's own aircrew accommodation. Nevertheless, accidents did happen, such as one incident at Graveley, when it is believed that an armourer accidentally triggered a delayed-action bomb fuse, blowing up one of the dumps and killing several men.

Transporting the bombs from the manufacturers to the airfields was particularly dangerous. Huntingdonshire's RAF bombs were delivered by truck from Cambridge. Cpl D.A.A. Radford was driving one such truck when another vehicle almost ran him off the road just outside Cambridge, on the old St Ives road: 'I lost one of the bombs off the trailer; it finished up in a ditch. The police cleared the surrounding area although I don't remember much housing there. I just sat and watched for a couple of armourers and a crane to come out and reload them.' A similar incident happened in Huntingdon High Street itself, when a bomb rolled off a lorry as it was turning next to The Three Tuns public house. In September 1940, an army lorry loaded with explosives skidded out of control at Bythorn, causing a huge fire, but luckily no one was hurt.

A 'cookie' bomb, at the Imperial War Museum, Duxford. The transportation and loading of these extremely large bombs onto aeroplanes occasionally caused accidents. (The authors)

PERSONAL BRAVERY

On Sunday 8 May 1944, at about 3.25 p.m., a Mosquito crashed into a cottage at Tetworth, killing its crew of two instantly. Fifty-two-year-old Jacob Lamb was sitting in his garden about 30 yards away when he saw the plane hit the cottage and explode. Without any hesitation Lamb ran to the burning cottage and rescued first Kathleen Gilbert and then her sister Mrs Miriam Gore, whose clothing was on fire. He placed her on the ground and extinguished the flames. After taking Mrs Gore to his own house he returned to the burning cottage, but it had collapsed in the meantime and he found it impossible to enter. 'Had it not been for the prompt action taken by Mr Lamb in all probability Mrs Gore would have lost her life,' the Chief Constable wrote in his report. Sadly, Miriam's husband Oliver, thirty-three, died in the explosion.

At 11.15 a.m. on 4 August 1944, an American Mustang fighter plane crashed into Cow Paddock at Sibson. The Mustang had taken off from USAAF Kings Cliffe on its way to Europe for a mission and was therefore fully loaded with ammunition. John Henry Tate, a seventy-five-year-old former special constable, saw the aircraft hit the ground from 150 yards away and immediately ran towards the burning wreck, undeterred by the exploding ammunition and roaring flames. He caught hold of the pilot and endeavoured to pull him out, but 'his gallantry was of no avail as the pilot was strapped in, and it was impossible to loosen the straps.' The pilot died, but Tate's heroism had been observed by witnesses and he received an official commendation, printed in the *London Gazette* in December.

CHAPTER 7

'Doing our Damndest': Digging for Victory in Huntingdonshire

Enemy blockades of British shipping lanes meant that it would be necessary to produce more food at home. A War Agricultural Executive Committee (WAEC) for Huntingdonshire was appointed in September 1939. In common with many other organisations, the WAEC was based at the old grammar school in Huntingdon. Their aim was to have an extra 5,000 acres under the plough by 31 December. A grant of £2 per acre for ploughing up land was available to farmers until March 1940, but by the end of October only 400 extra acres had been ploughed, using nine extra tractors. Farmers worked day and night to achieve the target. There were penalties for those who failed to comply. In July 1940, Frank Edwards of Red House Farm, Woodwalton was fined £20 for not ploughing up his grassland. John Williams from Catworth was fined the same amount in May 1942 for failing to plough up two fields.

By the end of 1941, the WAEC was employing 125 men and eighty women, plus forty-eight tractor drivers. Over 1,674 acres of bushed land had been cleared for production and sixty-eight farms, including Hardwicke Farm near Great Gransden and Sisman's Farm at Alconbury Weston, had been taken over by the WAEC. Huntingdonshire was a model example of how things should be done: the Minister for Agriculture and Fisheries, Mr R.S. Hudson, was so impressed after his visit in July 1941 that he returned a few weeks later with farmers from Bedfordshire, Buckinghamshire, Berkshire, Hertfordshire and Middlesex to show them what could be achieved. Much of the land cleared had been heavily bushed or semi-waterlogged heavy clay and ditches had become clogged up. A few months later, a group of US agriculturalists toured Huntingdonshire assessing the need for agricultural equipment which would be supplied as part of the lend-lease programme.

Gradually the area of land cultivated in Huntingdonshire increased. In 1931 there had been less than 30,000 acres of wheat, but by 1943 this had increased to over 47,000 acres. There had also been an increase in potato acreage from 3,000 to 15,000 acres. Portholme and Hemingford Meadow were under cultivation. By April 1943, the WAEC had taken over more than 8,000 acres of derelict land.

Left: A government publication on the advantages of allotments. (Cambridgeshire Libraries)

Below: Land workers in 1944. From left to right: junior land workers at Hail Weston; a wheat harvest at Bluntisham; plum picking at Bluntisham. (*Hunts Post*)

   The Minister for Agriculture maintained that the war would be won by the side which had the best civilian morale and no better contribution to morale could be made than to ensure adequate supplies of food. It was imperative to cut down on the amount of food imported to release shipping for other purposes. In 1942, the minister declared, 'This year's harvest may decide not only the outcome of the war but the fate of civilisation for generations to come.' That is how important feeding the nation had become. As with savings and salvage, the Government launched contests to encourage production. The 'Victory Churn Contest' of 1942–43 set up six regional milk leagues and offered prizes for the greatest increase in milk production. In June 1943, Huntingdonshire came top in the Eastern League and won a silver victory churn.

Many of those who worked on the land would be needed to fight, so recruiting of a Women's Land Army began early in the war. The response was poor, possibly because of the billeting of evacuees in the area. Major Proby of Elton, chairman of the War Agricultural Executive Committee, was one of those who supported the formation of a boy's land army. This was vetoed by the education authority, although boys did help out in the holidays. Maj. Proby had a camp at Elton Hall for farm workers who travelled to the farms each day. There was another camp behind Rectory Farm on the estate of Lord de Ramsey at Abbots Ripton. In August 1940, about forty scouts from all over the southern part of the county were staying there to help with the harvest. School summer holidays were taken in two parts to help with the harvest of potatoes. Great Paxton School closed for a fortnight in September 1940 for the potato and blackberry harvest. The following year, 1,100 troops were brought in for the potato harvest.

PRISONERS OF WAR

Prisoners of War were also employed harvesting potatoes, beet and carrots. By April 1942 there were 125 POWs working in the county, all but six working on private farms. Four farmers had applied for prisoners to 'live in.' Italian prisoners were also brought in to build roads around Yaxley for agricultural traffic and employed by the Ouse Catchment Board doing hedging and ditching. Those working in the gardens of the Huntingdonshire Public Assistance Institutions were paid 1s an hour. In some areas, gangs of outside workers were drafted in. These usually included a considerable number of conscientious objectors. In November 1942, 600 soldiers were brought into the county to help with ploughing and seeding wheat.

By 1943, the number of POWs, mainly Italians, helping on Huntingdonshire farms had risen to 500. Discipline was called into question when it was alleged that Italian POWs were calling each day at a local public house. Several land girls were fined for sending notes to Italian prisoners which had not been through the postal system (and the censor). On 21 May 1944 a police constable on duty saw an Italian POW carrying two sacks: the constable stopped him, and discovered some stolen ham and asparagus. More worrying was the fact that some POWs managed to get hold of weapons. In September 1944 Huntingdonshire Constabulary were notified that a member of the USAAF had allegedly been 'shot by two Italian POWs' in a secluded spot at Molesworth.

Fears about POWs appeared to have been justified when twenty-three-year-old Antonio Amedeo, who had been captured at Tobruk, escaped from a farm at Tilbrook on 9 July 1943. Amedeo attacked and killed the sentry with a hedge

Italian POWs working on the land. (Cambridgeshire Libraries: W.22 K.4 34222)

hook, almost decapitating him. He stole his rifle and ten rounds of ammunition, which he fired at a land girl, Rita Higgins, who ran away and raised the alarm. Police, the Home Guard and regular soldiers, together with two bloodhounds, joined the manhunt, searching all through the night. The prisoner was eventually discovered hiding at Grange Farm, Pertenhall. He fired at the Shelton family who lived at the farm, before being stalked through the farmhouse and shot dead by eighteen-year-old John Shelton, a member of the Home Guard.

Military labour dried up as troops were deployed on active service, so more and more POWs were drafted in as time went on. By October 1944 there were 1,265 working across Huntingdonshire. The number now included around 400 Germans, who were said to work four times harder than the Italians. The Germans were employed on the potato harvest in Ramsey Hollow and Ramsey Mereside. In Upwood village two German POWs worked for Lady Shepperson. They visited Mrs King's village shop for spare tobacco and were remembered as being very polite.

The treatment of these POWs caused a lot of resentment locally. It was felt that they had an easy life while our own troops were fighting and dying abroad. The letters pages of the *Hunts Post* contained many complaints about the 'good and favourable treatment' of the Italians. Several of these letters were received from Huntingdonshire soldiers serving abroad. It was said that Italian prisoners had been billeted in a 'fine residence' in Bury Road Ramsey, while suitable

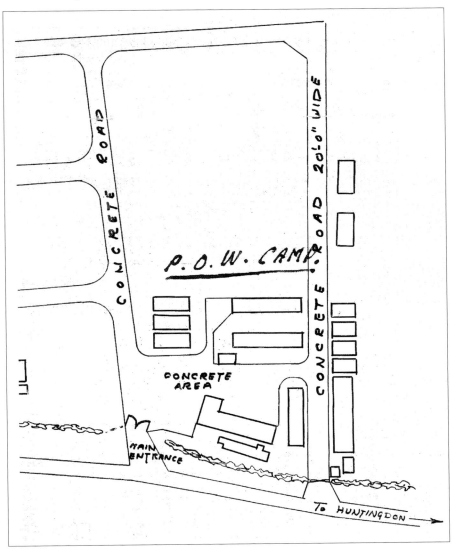

Plan of the POW camp on St Peter's Road in Huntingdon. (County Record Office Huntingdon: 3830)

accommodation for civilians was unavailable. It was suggested that empty huts in Cemetery Road would be more suitable lodgings for them. Another house in Huntingdon Street, St Neots, requisitioned by the War Office, which the UDC had been trying to obtain for evacuees, was refurbished and used for Italian prisoners. The fact was that Italians who had agreed to co-operate with the war effort and whose work was satisfactory were allowed considerable freedom. They were allowed to exercise within five miles of their camps, visit shops and cinemas and

Prisoners of War, probably Italian, watching a football match during the 1940s.
(Cambridgeshire Libraries: S.194 14846)

talk to civilians, although 'fraternization of an amorous nature' was strictly forbidden. After Italy declared war on Germany, the treatment of POWs was eased still further. Batches of prisoners were often seen roaming the streets of Ramsey. In fact there were so many Italians in the district that a visiting circus displayed its opening times in English and Italian. Despite protests, Italians were even attending whist drives in Grafham.

By 1945, there were sixteen POW camps in Huntingdonshire, such as the one in Woodwalton Lane, Sawtry, housing about 1,350 Germans and 530 Italians. Another 260 Italians were billeted on farms. 500 more Germans were expected in Yaxley in September. By the end of 1945 around 3,000 POWs were working in the county. A few were working in industry and twelve Germans were helping with house building in Sawtry, but the majority were working on farms.

THE WOMEN'S LAND ARMY

As time went on, the Women's Land Army (WLA) began to flourish. There were hostels at Elton Cottage, Woolley Rectory, Love's Farm in St Neots and Hiam's Farm, part of Dr Gregory's estate at Houghton. The twenty-four girls at Hiam's Farm in 1941 were all from Yorkshire. Those working in the county came from all walks of life. Miss Sylvia Bosley, a London sculptress before the war was driving a tractor and several former actresses were also working on the land, from 7.00 a.m. until 6.00 p.m. Mrs Haynes and Miss Saxty joined the WLA too, having had experience from working as land girls in the First World War. In April 1942, there were ninety-four WLA members and ten other women working in the county. Additional hostels had opened at Stilton Cottage and Sawtry and another at Catworth was planned. In August 1943, fifty land girls from Yorkshire were billeted at The Hall in Great Gransden, formerly occupied by pupils from Hornsey High School. By 1944, there was a further hostel at Fenstanton. Sylvia Bosley worked in Huntingdonshire for six years, moving on from driving and servicing tractors to being in charge of the girls at Hardwick Farm, Great Gransden. She later became assistant cultivations officer and ran courses at Buckden Towers. At the end of the war she was awarded the British Empire Medal.

Numbers in the WLA increased steadily as time went on. By 1943 there were 254 women working in Huntingdonshire. Some had gained specialist qualifications in loading straw, thatching, milking and tractor driving. Proficiency tests were held at Mill Farm, Great Gidding.

Woolley Lodge, which had been disused and run down before the war, was requisitioned and done up by the WAEC. Initially, it was used as a centre for tractor driving courses. Students learnt about different types of farm machinery from experts who were brought in from as far afield as London. The wardens at Woolley Lodge, Mr and Mrs Brindley, looked after the students. Following the success of these courses, further courses of instruction were run by the WEAC for the WLA girls. Those who passed them received a higher rate of pay. A series of courses were held at Buckden Towers. One of the subjects covered was 'rat destruction' although thousands had already been caught and killed. Girls from the WLA were routinely doing this job.

Life in the WLA was not easy. The women worked out in the fields all day. There was no canteen for hot meals and tea for them, they had to make do with sandwiches under the hedge. The WLA girls did find some time to relax though. At Hiam's Farm they organised a weekly 'Hippodrome' with music and dancing. There were also facilities to enable them to play darts and table tennis.

The next scheme was for a 'Women's Land Workers Corps', organised by Mrs Proby. Women who had other commitments were asked to work part-time on the land or help out when extra labour was required in their own localities. There was to be a local representative in each village. The *Hunts Post* wrote that: 'by joining the Corps women will be performing an essential national service and may be instrumental in saving much valuable food which would otherwise be lost for lack of labour at the right time.' The scheme was a success and by July 1942, 500 women had enrolled in the Women's Land Corps.

Other men and women who worked full-time spent the summer evenings helping out, picking strawberries and peas. The WAEC organised nightly fruit picking excursions from Huntingdon to Colne, Somersham and Bluntisham. A bus left the Market Square at 5.30 p.m. each evening, taking about forty men and women – most of whom had been working in offices all day – for three hours open-air work in the fields. There was only one recorded case of anyone becoming ill from eating too much fruit! Once the harvest was in full swing, office workers were being taken in open and closed lorries to anywhere help was needed – strawberry picking at Mr Fred Noble's farm at Pidley; pea picking at Mr Rose's farm in Bluntisham; haymaking at Mr How's in Bluntisham; poppy pulling at Stukeley and thinning out sugar beet at Home Farm, Brampton. At

Queen Marie of Yugoslavia inspects members of the Women's Land Army at the New Grammar School in Huntingdon, in March 1943. (*Hunts Post*)

Noble's farm, evacuees kept pickers supplied with baskets. Mr Noble sent his helpers home with gifts of cherries in return for their three hours work. Once the evenings began to get dark, the lorries left Huntingdon at 2.15 p.m. and work finished at 7 p.m. In 1943, as many as 144 helpers left Huntingdon on a single night. The same year, USAAF troops were also helping out with the harvest. This was a bonus as they not only refused payment for their services, but also provided their own transport. The WI and WVS did their bit, of course, providing 'harvest canteens' for the workers at thirty key centres like Somersham, Colne and Fenstanton. By the end of the summer about 500 workers were benefiting from the canteens which provided meat pasties, sausage and ham rolls and bacon sandwiches.

Between 1943 and 1945, there were volunteer camps for adults at Buckden Towers, with space for 100 adults and 100 boys, aged fifteen to seventeen. People came from as far away as Liverpool and London. The volunteers were accommodated in tents in the grounds. They rose at 7 a.m., breakfasted at eight and left for farms within a ten-mile radius, taking a packed lunch. The work included harvesting, pea picking, fruit picking and hay making. They were paid 1s per hour per day. Workers would return at 8 p.m. Dances were held each week for the workers at the rifle range. In 1944, there were 1,621 volunteers who put in 43,850

Women's Land Army lorry at Huntingdon, 1944. (*Hunts Post*)

working hours over a fifteen-week season. Many had come from areas targeted by flying bombs.

GROWING YOUR OWN FOOD

People in rural areas often did better under rationing than those in urban areas. Rural gardens were bigger; there were more allotments and a wider choice of wild-life to kill. Ducks were quite rare during the war, as any duck foolish enough to be outside in daylight was likely to end up in someone's kitchen. Children would go into the countryside and collect mushrooms and capture rabbits to make pies. By 1942, many families in the country had become poultry-keepers, keeping birds in makeshift hen houses behind their homes. Villagers and allotment holders were also encouraged to keep pigs. The village of Wintringham near St Neots, with a popula-tion of only twenty-three, had a pig club with eight pigs, beating all the other clubs in England with bacon production per head of population. Across Huntingdonshire as a whole, there were thirteen co-operative pig clubs and fourteen private owner clubs with around 1,000 members altogether. About 1,500 pigs a year were killed for members' consumption and another 1,000 for the general meat market.

Harvest help cartoon from the *Hunts Post*, July 1945.

Rabbits also became a popular meal. The first Domestic Rabbit & Poultry Club was formed at St Ives in November 1941 with sixty members. This was soon followed by a club in Huntingdon. Huntingdon & District Domestic Rabbit & Poultry Club had 100 members and in 1943 alone sent 1,132 animals to the butchers, ninety to Hinchingbrooke Convalescent Home and seventeen to the county hospital.

Local schools set up young farmers clubs. At Kimbolton, they kept pigs, poultry, goats and rabbits, as well as growing vegetables. The tennis courts at Huntingdon Grammar School were used for hay and transformed into allotments. In 1942, pupils at Kimbolton, Huntingdon Grammar and Tollington (evacuated to Buckden) school pupils were taking lessons in tractor driving so they could help with the ploughing.

Private gardens were also dug up – the spacious lawn of Rheola in St Ives was transformed into a kitchen garden. As time went on, more land was used for food

Above left: Hermann and Benito, two pigs kept by pupils at Kings Ripton School, 1941.
(*Hunts Post*)

Above right: Advert for selling on fruit surplus, from the *Hunts Post*, August 1943.

production. Trenches dug in the panic of 1940 at Kimbolton School were filled in two years later and used for cultivation. At the end of 1942, 10 acres of St Neots Golf Club was dug up to grow potatoes. Surplus land at RAF stations was also used for cultivation. Private gardens were inspected to make sure they were properly cultivated.

War was waged on pests. A price was put on the heads and eggs of house sparrows – 3*d* per dozen for heads and 2*d* per dozen for eggs. 1*d* was paid for each rat tail collected. By April 1940, 19,471 rats' tails and 3,000 sparrows' heads had been handed in. Rookeries and wood pigeons' nests were destroyed. Butterflies were also killed. Children were paid 4*d* per 100 cabbage white butterflies and 263,850 had been traded in by the end of October 1940, costing the Hunts WAEC £39 16*s* 2*d*.

There was an all-out campaign to preserve fruit and vegetables for winter use. In July 1940, the Hunts Federation of Women's Institutes purchased a canning machine for use in the county. The first use of the machine saw eighty tins of gooseberries canned at the house of Mrs Gush in Brampton. The following year, four canning machines, gifts from America, were available for use in the county, mainly canning tomatoes. There was a machine in Huntingdon, one in Ramsey, one in Buckden and the fourth available for other areas.

In July 1940, a co-operative fruit preservation centre was opened by Ramsey WI. In just two weeks, 950lb of jam were made at the WI Hall. Revd P.J. Turner loaned the Vicarage in Upwood as a jam-making centre. Over the summer of 1940, an amazing 2,972lb of jam were made at Sawtry, despite a shortage of soft fruit due to bad weather. Ramblers and cyclists were urged to help out by collecting wild blackberries. Over 50lb of blackberries were gathered at St Ives. They were sold in aid of the Spitfire Fund. There were very strict controls on the use of the sugar supplied for jam making. One Sawtry woman was fined for giving 4lb of her allowance away as a wedding present.

During the 1941 jam-making season, much resentment was caused by the appointment of a paid supervisor to check the quality of the jam. Most WI members objected to having their jam-making skills checked. Amounts of jam made fell, largely due to a shortage of fruit again caused by bad weather. Only thirty out of seventy registered centres operated. Out of 6,000lb of jam produced, 2,000lb were made by Staughton WI. These thirty jam-making centres made 14,727lb of jam in 1942, operating in places such as a disused garage, a barn and an old laundry.

Employees of Chivers gave up their Sundays to ensure continuous food production, processing peas and other vegetables for canning. The canning and drying operation in Huntingdon was inspected by Government minister, Lord Woolton, in May 1943. At this time, all the output was being sent off to British troops and POWs.

COMMUNAL DINING

The purpose of British restaurants was to allow everyone access to good food at affordable prices. They were run on a 'not-for-profit' basis and were mainly found in towns and industrial areas. A British restaurant was set up in Trinity church schoolroom in Huntingdon. This had been intended as a communal feeding centre for evacuees only, but was soon opened to all as a British restaurant, under the supervision of Mrs Riley. In the early days, about twenty-five customers a day were enjoying a two-course meal for 8*d* (children 5*d*), but by 1942 it was serving 300 meals a day. In 1944, Mrs Robinson became the first paid manageress.

Godmanchester councillors opposed the setting up of a British restaurant, arguing that people could simply walk to Huntingdon. They thought it would be

Huntingdon's Mayor, Cllr Maddox, at the British Restaurant in Huntingdon, December 1941. (*Hunts Post*)

too expensive and make too much work for the volunteers. The restaurant would 'simply be catering to the idleness of people who are too lazy to get their own meals', they declared.

In May 1942 Molesworth received a communal feeding centre too. This was a 'cash-and-carry' restaurant, the first of its type in a Huntingdonshire village. It was run by seventy-year-old Mrs Penzer and a team of volunteers. The kitchen was equipped by the Ministry of Food for less than £30. It was installed in a small outhouse attached to a cottage and supplied fifty hot meals, three times a week. Initially this was a takeaway service only, but such was the demand that, in 1943, a hut was erected to serve meals on the premises.

During the summer of 1941, the WI and WVS joined forces to provide harvest meals for the extra workers engaged in bringing in the harvest. This was so successful that plans were made to carry on the scheme through the winter for local people. The process was inevitably a slow one: discussions were held and committees formed. The harvest canteen at Colne was the first to reopen, supplying cooked meat, pasties and fried fish to local workers. Waterloo Farm was to serve as the canteen for Abbotsley. By 1942, sixty-two villages had registered with what became the Huntingdonshire Rural Meals Scheme (popularly known as the 'pie scheme'). Steak pies, pork pies, meat flans, sausages, brawn and so on were made communally to be collected from a designated centre at set times, usually once a week in smaller villages. The scheme was designed to supplement normal rations and was particularly aimed at agricultural workers, giving them the same opportunities as those in towns. By July 1942, there were eighty such distribution centres serving more than 5,000 customers.

CHAPTER 8

'Stout Hearts': Soldiers in Huntingdonshire

Soldiers were to be found all across Huntingdonshire. One particularly large group was based in Hartford, in a camp made up of Nissen huts near the village hall. The soldiers were equipped with tanks and Ray Smith later recalled the soldiers taking their tanks down to the river to wash them. He, and the other boys, would sneak up and pinch the scrubbing brushes and later return these 'lost' brushes to the guardroom at the King of the Belgians pub, where they would be given a slice of corned beef as a reward. The soldier's huts in Hartford were later used to house enemy POWs.

The King's Own Scottish Borderers were billeted in Nissen huts at Somersham Rectory. The troops marched down Somersham High Street each morning at 7.30 a.m. towards the Palace Hall, accompanied by bagpipes. After D-Day, these huts were also used for POWs and so too were the huts of Diddington Camp, which also saw life as an army camp, a hospital, an evacuation hospital for Americans and, after the war, a recuperation centre for Polish soldiers. Other large detachments of troops manned anti-aircraft posts and searchlights, including positions at Rowell's Farm in Tick Fen, Warboys; Collingwood Farm on St Audrey Lane, St Ives; North Fen, Somersham; the Bulwark, Earith and Park Farm in Ramsey.

FEEDING THE TROOPS

Many villages had made an effort to provide recreation for the evacuees, but they were not the only ones needing entertainment through the blackout. As troops arrived in the towns, they too needed entertaining and feeding.

In Huntingdon, the Territorial Hut in St Mary's Street was acquired as a troops' canteen and recreation centre and was renamed the Military Social Club. From November 1939 it was open each evening from 6 p.m. until 10 p.m. It provided a billiard table, table tennis, bagatelle, a card room and a reading and writing room. Elphicks loaned a piano. When it opened, 120 men were expected, but hardly anyone turned up. A lone RAF man had to enlist three helpers to make up a

Sgt Fred Edwards of Somersham at Buckingham Palace, November 1944. Sgt Edwards received the Military Medal and Bar for gallantry in the Western Desert. (*Hunts Post*)

four for snooker! The centre grew in popularity though, and at its peak served 500 servicemen in one evening. The Huntingdon Model Laundry did all the canteen's washing free of charge. As well as entertaining the troops, the services canteen managed to make a profit of £1,000, which was donated to good causes.

In Ramsey, the Salvation Army began opening their hall as a canteen and social centre for service men each evening, except Wednesday and Sunday, from 6 p.m. to 9 p.m. Two rooms at the Liberal Club on the Market Square in St Neots were used for the same purpose, with all the usual facilities: table tennis, reading room, tea, coffee, Oxo, bread and butter, biscuits, cake, sandwiches, chocolates and cigarettes being provided. Initially, this canteen was serving 200 meals a week, but by January 1942 it was serving between 7,000 and 8,000 and had to move to new premises in the Market Square. The services canteen in the Market Square in St Neots was open daily from 9 a.m. to 10 p.m. and vehicles of all kinds were constantly parked outside it. It was still serving around 8,500 hot drinks and 7,500 meals a week in 1944. The Methodist Schoolroom in Huntingdon Street, St Neots was also opened as a canteen and rest room for members of HM Forces.

WVS canteens were also serving vast quantities of food. In Ramsey, the WVS canteen was established in the WI Hall in June 1940 before moving to the Drill Hall. By the autumn of 1942, the Drill Hall was required by the Home Guard, so the canteen moved again, this time to the Abbey Rooms. In its first year, the canteen served 41,999 meals. By 1941-42 this had risen to 72,079. There were about thirty helpers working there. Another services canteen opened at the 'White Hart' in Warboys. Run by the WVS, it was open to all service personnel between

A parade in Station Road and Market Road, St Ives, looking from Market Hill towards the railway station, showing Scotney's Canteen. A contingent of RAF personnel is turning out of Station Road into Market Road, carrying rifles at the high port and all with respirators slung; a civilian band is behind them in Station Road. (Norris Museum: PH/S.IVE/Markets/12)

6 p.m. and 9.30 p.m. Yet another services canteen opened at Great Staughton in April 1944.

The most famous such canteen was Scotneys in St Ives. A new hut was erected in the cattle market, provided and equipped by Tom Scotney for troops' recreation. Men from the Royal Fusiliers and the Royal Army Medical Corps were the first to use it when it opened on 1 June 1940. Refreshments were provided by a ladies committee. Just over two weeks after opening, they entertained nearly 400 soldiers evacuated from Dunkirk two days running. They arrived between 10.30 p.m. and 1.30 a.m. Volunteers stayed on to cater for them and were then up serving breakfast at 7 a.m.

One of the first soldiers to use Scotney's commented: 'Blimey, it looks like an officers' mess!' Scotney's canteen became one of the most well-used centres for troops in Huntingdonshire. In the first two years of operation, 214,000 men used the facilities. When it finally closed, in October 1945, a social was held for all the staff, helpers and committee and its equipment was then auctioned off.

A YMCA canteen and hostel opened in Huntingdon, opposite the Methodist church on 11 December 1941. There was a canteen on the ground floor and a sleeping area with ten double-tier bunks on the first floor. Also on the first floor was a lounge and reading room. A third room was used for games or more bunks as required. One of the main attractions was the three hot-shower baths and a number of washbasins available in a room at the back of the premises. At its peak, the canteen was serving up to 1,000 cups of tea per day. The YMCA canteen was the last of the servicemen's clubs to remain open after the war.

The Literary Institute was also used as a recreation centre for the troops in Huntingdon. Its basement had been adapted for use as a public air-raid shelter, although this did not finally become available until 1941 due to wrangling about the laying of reinforced concrete and who would pay to have it removed after the war. During the Blitz, rooms at the Trinity church schoolroom were regularly lined with mattresses and people had to sleep on the stage. Four bedrooms were used by service girls or visiting wives.

ENTERTAINING THE TROOPS

The ladies of the WVS were tireless in their efforts to make things easier for those serving in the forces. Each time a trainload of soldiers arrived at Huntingdon station they would be on duty serving coffee, sandwiches and buns, no matter what time of day.

From February 1941 onwards, Lucy Boston held a regular series of gramophone concerts for servicemen at her home, Hemingford Grey Manor House. The gramophone player itself was hand-wound, with an immense horn and the thorn needles needed changing every record. Someone would be given the task of continually winding the player while the others sat in the music room, listening to the music. The *Enigma Variations* was a popular choice, as was the *St Anthony*

Mr Scotney (centre) stands outside his welfare canteen for the troops, June 1940. (*Hunts Post*)

Chorale. The concerts began simply, with a few RAF aircrew from Wyton, but soon they became well-established and popular.

Dances were regularly held for locals and troops stationed in the county. In the Corn Exchange at St Ives, soldiers attending the dances were issued with plimsolls because their boots damaged the floor. In Ramsey, weekly dances were held on Fridays and Saturdays in the WI Hall. On Tuesdays, dances were held in the Abbey Rooms for Mrs Pilkington's cigarette fund and at the same venue on Thursdays for other causes. In April 1942, the conga was danced for the first time in Huntingdon at the Fireman's Annual Dance in the Town Hall. From January 1942, numbers at the weekly dances at the Town Hall in Huntingdon had to be limited to 200 as it was becoming too crowded.

Special efforts were made at Christmas. For example, troops on active service near the village of Wistow were entertained at the Manor House to a roast beef dinner, followed by plum pudding, mince pies, trifle, cheese, celery and biscuits, cigarettes, coffee and beer. A band played throughout and there were songs, conjuring tricks and darts all through the evening. At the services canteen in St Mary's Street no charge was made for food, drink, cigarettes and billiards on Christmas night. Refreshments were also free on New Year's Eve. The coming year was toasted with lemonade.

As anti-aircraft posts were set up, often in remote areas, appeals were made for lamps, books and games for the men stationed there. The WVS co-ordinated the appeal, which was extended to include footballs, table-tennis tables, gramophone records and, later, musical instruments and bicycles. By the end of 1940, each of these remote sites had a furnished recreation hut provided by the WVS. In September 1940, a mobile snack bar was started up for men in AA and searchlight detachments. It was based at the old grammar school in Huntingdon. Two ladies from London, Miss Adshead and Mrs Stephen, took it round the county, towed by Miss Adshead's own car. This mobile canteen even visited the searchlight sites on Christmas Day and Boxing Day.

In addition to a full programme of major films at local cinemas, which began to open on Sundays despite fierce opposition in some quarters, the people of Huntingdonshire could also amuse themselves with films supplied by the Ministry of Information. These toured the region and in 1942 the MOI screened over 3,600 shows in the eastern region. There were over 200 different films available, including five about Russia. Each show consisted of a mix of films, usually one about the armed forces, one about the needs of the moment (war saving, salvage, digging for victory and so on) and one about Britain's industrial output.

Due to the fear of invasion and the difficulties of travelling, local councils advocated 'holidays at home'. Special weeks of activities were held, such as the games week at Slepe Hall in St Ives which featured rounders, netball, tenniquoit, volleyball and handball. In Huntingdon, the council spent £18 on the construction of concrete sandpits at Hartford Road playing fields, Mill Common and in Cowper Road. These proved popular with local children, who used spoons and forks to

The Spotlights Concert Party performing *Going Up* in Huntingdon, 1942. (County Record Office Huntingdon: 1598 part)

Members of the American Red Cross visit the George Hotel in the 1940s. (County Record Office Huntingdon: 3521/12)

build sandcastles. A further sandpit was constructed on Spring Common. Beaches, even if you could get to them, were covered with anti-invasion defences.

Local clubs and societies continued to operate and many of these welcomed members of the forces. The Railway Inn Bowls Club at Ramsey, for example, introduced a special monthly subscription for members of the forces.

Children enjoying the 'holidays at home' sandpits in Hartford Road, Huntingdon. (*Hunts Post*)

FOREIGN TROOPS

After 1941, British troops had been joined in Huntingdonshire by troops arriving from America. Late in 1942, it was decided that the US NCOs and men needed their own recreation club. The Freemasons offered the use of their headquarters, the Priory, in Huntingdon. They even left their billiard table for the troops to use. The club would have forty to fifty beds, showers, a snack bar, games room and information bureau. It was run by the American Red Cross, aided by local volunteers. Needless to say, a committee was set up – the Hunts Entertainment & Welfare Committee for US Troops – with Lord Sandwich as president. Lady Sandwich was also particularly interested in the project, being American by birth. The club was officially opened on 21 October 1942, by which time men from thirty-one different US states had signed in.

The US Red Cross Club gave a party each month for those soldiers and members of staff whose birthday fell in that month. The premises later became too small to meet demand and a further centre was opened in Hodges Close. The US Forces Club at the Priory was just one of the local venues visited by a group of Hollywood stars, Fay Raye, Kay Francis, Carole Londis and Mitzi Mayfair, who were touring US army camps and naval bases.

Army concert parties, such as the Blue Pencils, often appeared at local venues. The Blue Pencils were well known for featuring the 'can-can' in their repertoire. In July 1944, noted American 'artistes' were in concert at Huntingdon Town Hall. Cpl Myron Klempner, a concert pianist from Manhattan and S/Sgt Barton Mumaw, the leading male dancer in the US, described by the local newspaper as 'a young man with the figure of a Greek god whose every movement was a poem of exquisite grace and beauty', performed together with an American male voice trio and local performers. The *Hunts Post* considered that, under normal circumstances, a small market town like Huntingdon could have waited a century and not seen performers of such quality.

Soldiers from other countries were made equally welcome. In October 1943 forty Czech soldiers were entertained at a party at the church hall in Godmanchester, organised by the vicar and churchwardens. The Czech soldiers gave a demonstration of potato cookery: the soldiers, some of whom had been professional chefs, produced three courses with potato as the main ingredient. They did this in appreciation of the kindness shown to them by the people of Godmanchester. In December 1943 Czech officers and their wives were invited to view Godmanchester's Royal Charters.

Czech forces also organised a table-tennis camp at Huntingdon Town Hall in December 1943. There was a table-tennis exhibition, where Czech players of national standard showed off their skills. There were appeals for Huntingdonshire people to entertain the Czech troops over Christmas – there would be no parcels from home for them!

Parties were organized for the Czechs every Monday at the Buckden Rifle Range. Czech soldiers were welcomed at the Huntingdon Services Club. The club's annual report refers to them as, 'Loyal and homeless men ... [they] were greatly appreciated by everyone at the club ... [who had] quite fallen in love with their Czech friends.'

A concert party at RAF Wyton. (Jean Matthews)

A Czech's View of Huntingdon

The following lines were written by one of the Czech soldiers who were at one time stationed in the Huntingdon district : —

A dreaming river and smiling girls,
Birthplace of Cromwell. seat of
*   Earls.*
Narrow old lane. and a traffic jam;
Salami and sausage; no eggs, no
*   ham.*
A Service Canteen and laughing
*   W.A.A.F's,*
And "Stars" and "Wings" and
*   Czechs and R.A.F.s.*
Bombers from battle droning
*   home—*
And boys below talking of Lvov
*   and Rome. . . .*
The people — stout hearts. free,
*   friendly and tough;*
The place seems to be made of
*   Cromwell stuff.*
And what we the Czechs agree
*   upon*
We had a grand feeling here
*   —being at home.*
Let this be a message from friend
*   to friend.*
Let it be like this to the victorious
*   end!*
Let's deepen our friendship after
*   the war—*
Pact signed; Huntingdon, May.
*   forty and four.*

A poem written by a Czech soldier in Huntingdonshire, published in the *Hunts Post* on 6 July 1944.

GAYNES HALL

Local people knew all about the soldiers and airmen living in Huntingdonshire, but there were other things going on which were kept top secret. Tempsford Airfield near St Neots was chosen as HQ for a special RAF squadron which was formed to ferry agents and drop supplies into occupied Europe. Before leaving on their missions, the agents would wait at Gaynes Hall, living in temporary luxury, with no shortage of food, drink or entertainment. On the night before a drop the agent would be given two fried eggs on a warm plate, a simple tribute by the staff who recognised the dangers these brave people would be exposed to.

Agents from various European countries passed through Gaynes Hall, including Odette and Peter Churchill and Wg Cdr F.Yeo Thomas, the famous 'White Rabbit'. No one knew who anyone else was nor where they would be going. Local civilians were not allowed anywhere near Gaynes Hall: guards were told to shoot first and ask questions afterwards and all the staff at the hall were hand-picked, even the charwoman.

CHAPTER 9

'Tea and Warm Beer': Americans in Huntingdonshire

The US military arrived in Huntingdonshire only a few weeks after the American declaration of war on Germany in December 1941. In February 1942, American Army Air Force officers visited Huntingdonshire to assess the suitability of some of its RAF airfields for use by their own bombers. RAF Molesworth was one of the fields selected. The airfield at Molesworth had been built during the winter of 1940–41, but until 1942 it only had been a temporary home for numerous squadrons, including a Hawker Hurricane fighter training unit (No.5 Flying Training School) and an Australian squadron which flew Wellington bombers. No unit had been based there permanently. The Americans extended Molesworth's runways and built more accommodation and, on 9 June 1942, the first USAAF unit moved in. The 1st Bombardment Wing Headquarters was the first of its kind to be established at Brampton Grange, previously the headquarters of 7 Group RAF. The Grange was not big enough, so Brampton Park was taken over too. A large Nissen hut was erected behind Brampton Park for use as a dining hall and another was used as the Red Cross Aero Club. Even so, to begin with, most men were still living in tents. GI Frank Baker recalled: 'we basically lived in four-man tents that had been erected in the park. We had cots, but one could not even stand upright... we ate in the open from a field kitchen and I remember a lot of mutton, which nobody ate.'

RELATIONS WITH THE LOCALS

The Americans were popular with Huntingdonshire's residents, as they seemed interesting and exotic and often treated locals to food and sweets which they could not get any other way, due to the strict rationing in force. Margaret Faulkner was a child in Great Stukeley during the war years and remembered that her favourite Yank was a man called Seniors, who 'had the ability to make me laugh until I cried, which to be honest wasn't hard to do, but he had a way of saying things in exactly the way that set me off giggling.' One warm summer evening there was a knock on the back door:

USAAF personnel at Alconbury. (County Record Office Huntingdon: 4336/2 part)

The Grange Hotel in Brampton, which was HQ of the 1st Air Division of the US 8th Air Force. (The authors)

On opening it, Mum was delighted to find Seniors and a colleague standing there
with several plates in their arms. They swept into our kitchen and with a flourish
removed the napkins to reveal plates piled high with cold chicken salad, potato salad
and even bread rolls and butter. There was one for each of us. It appeared that during a dinner party for the Officers, an opportunity had arisen for Seniors to 'liberate'
some spare meals for his English friends. It was such a treat for us, all the more so for
being unexpected... We only had chicken on high days and holidays, so it was even
more of a treat than it would be today.

In return, Huntingdonshire's locals would provide services like doing the GIs'
laundry, or simply being happy to chat with the Americans from time to time and
to let them into their homes, all of which must have eased their homesickness.
Villagers at Broughton, for example, invited US servicemen into their homes for
tea. Frank Baker wrote 'my recollection is one of good feelings and an easy going
attitude between the GIs and the locals. We learned to drink tea and warm beer
and shared our post exchange rations with those around us.' Wounded American
servicemen from Cambridgeshire hospitals regularly visited Hemingford Grey
and Hemingford Abbots. They were entertained at different houses with gardens
by the river and given boat trips, while tea was provided at the Boathouse by Mr
and Mrs Giddins.

What the Americans threw out into the rubbish was often combed through for
items of financial worth by locals. Even the wooden cases in which the American
equipment was delivered had some value on the black market. 'They were made
of a fine thick seasoned timber,' Eric Davies of St Neots later recalled, 'the like of
which had not been available in Britain for some years and many residents took
advantage of the opportunity to collect a quantity of valuable wood for about £1
per lorry load'.

Not everyone was enamoured with the Americans. Lucy Boston of Hemingford
Grey preferred the German and Italian POWs to the Americans, especially 'the
GIs one saw about in Cambridge, with their arrogant ox-like faces chewing the
gum and their off-pink trousers tight over projecting bums.' Relations between
USAAF airmen and their English counterparts could also go badly. During the
summer of 1942, while the airfield at RAF Molesworth was still being converted to
American use, a cricket match was held at Huntingdon between two RAF teams.
The scorer was a USAAF man, chosen perhaps for impartiality. Unfortunately he
fell asleep and the game ended in a punch-up.

The Americans were more interested in baseball. The Molesworth team, which
won the 8th Air Force championship in 1943, often appeared in charity matches:
one game in Northampton drew 7,500 spectators. Members of the US forces
played baseball on Warner's Park in St Ives and basketball at the Corn Exchange.
US airmen from Glatton taught local boys how to play American football and a
US army captain was asked to present the prizes at Ramsey Abbey sports day.

THE YANKS VISIT HUNTINGDON.

Left: A cartoon published in the *Hunts Post* in June 1945 about the impact of the Americans in Huntingdon.

Below: Wounded US troops being entertained at Abbots Ripton Hall, the home of Lady de Ramsey, May 1945. (*Hunts Post*)

The Americans knew how to put on a good show at Christmas. Many USAAF airbases staged Christmas parties for the children in their area: the Americans at Molesworth, for instance, held a series of parties for local children during December 1942, providing them with previously unseen luxuries like bananas and ice cream. For the 1943 Christmas Eve party Santa Claus himself landed at Molesworth (in a B17 bomber rather than a sleigh, however) to greet the local children. A similar party was held there on 22 December 1944, with more than £100 being spent on food and entertainments.

Their colleagues at Alconbury laid on a tremendous spread of food at their Christmas party, which much have overwhelmed the local children used to rationing:

> There were slices of cold roast chicken, ham, corned beef (lean and delicious and not at all like we were used to). There were chips, hot potatoes, potato salad, hot vegetables, cold salad, cheeses, hot dogs, and piles of delicious bread, spread thickly with real butter (a whole week's ration on one slice!). Then there were the cakes, lemon meringue pie, fruit salads with tiny little marshmallows in it, doughnuts, creamy ice cream and frosted Christmas cakes made out of a light and fluffy sponge, not like the heavy fruit cakes our mothers had been saving their dried fruits for months to make. To wash it down we had the choice of lemonade, orange juice, milk or a curious fizzy brown drink in an odd-shaped bottle that they called 'coke', which was something completely new to us.

To top it all, the children were allowed to go back for seconds and thirds. At the party, Huntingdonshire schoolgirl Margaret Faulkner met an American called Walter and exchanged some letters with him. Then a few weeks later one of her letters was returned, with a note explaining that Walter had been killed in action. 'I was very upset and thought then, as I do now, that to die in that little Perspex bubble at the rear of the plane, must have been sheer hell.'

It was widely believed that life expectancy for the American bomber crews was about six weeks. I.B. Hunter later recalled:

> I saw several American planes during the day, all shot up with bullet holes, and with damaged tails. A friend from school, who lived at Abbots Ripton, told me that the B17s from Alconbury passed extremely close to his house, so close that the pilots used to wave to him... I met such a pilot who actually told my sister the day he would die. A telephone call from the base to my sister informing her that he was missing was exact to the day. This has remained strong in my memory, and nearly every year I go to the American Cemetery at Madingly, Cambridge, and salute Flt Lt McKenna, who has no known grave, and all the fine Amerians who gave their lives for this country.

A US soldier is given a lesson in bowls at the Red Cross Club in the Priory, Huntingdon, April 1943. (*Hunts Post*)

American military and Red Cross personnel outside the George Hotel in Huntingdon. (County Record Office Huntingdon: 3521/7)

OVERPAID, OVERSEXED AND OVER HERE!

The USAAF airmen rarely organised any events which did not involve bringing local women onto the airbases. The St Patrick's Day party at Molesworth in 1944, for example, involved getting a large number of girls from local towns and villages into the airbase, as well as members of Britain's Women's Auxiliary Air Force (WAAFs). For an evening dance on 24 September 1944 the Americans at Molesworth even organised a fleet of buses to bring women from neighbouring towns onto the base, the buses picking up girls from as far afield as Bedford, Kettering, Northampton and Thrapston.

In October 1944, the 303rd Bombardment Group, based at Molesworth, declared a number of establishments off-limits to all US military personnel. As well as pubs with bad reputations, the locations included 'the home of Miss Ethel May Horne', in Old Weston Road, Winwick; and 115 High Street, Huntingdon. USAAF Molesworth held a beauty and dancing contest on 27 February 1945, at which the two winners, Doreen Williamson and Joan Eagle, had bombers named after them.

Many Huntingdonshire girls became GI brides, marrying their American boyfriends and then sailing with them to America to start a new life. Remarkably, USAAF Molesworth generated more marriages between Americans and local

The artwork on the fuselage side of *Alabama Bound* at Alconbury. The paintings on the sides of American bombers were occasionally based on local women. (County Record Office Huntingdon: 4336/2 part)

USAAF personnel at Alconbury. (County Record Office Huntingdon: 4336/2 part)

girls than any other airbase in the whole of England: 400 in all, easily beating USAAF Polebrook (with a paltry 250) into second place.

Americans were not the only ones marrying local women, of course. Several Czech soldiers had married local girls, so there would be ties with Huntingdon for many of them, even after the war. In general there were fears about the general relaxation of morals which seemed to be occurring during wartime. Many people felt that the appointment of women police officers, for example, would help to prevent the shocking decline in morals in Huntingdonshire towns which, according to the *Hunts Post*, was due to shameless young women 'enticing' young soldiers into 'foolishness'. A St Ives curate condemned the frequent dances held in the town as little better than 'orgies'.

THE BOMBING STRATEGY

American strategy was to bomb German-occupied Europe during the daytime, but these first Americans at Molesworth only had small Douglas A-20 bombers, which were unsuitable for the dangers of daylight bombing. The British sent fighters up each day to train the new USAAF bomber crews in procedures for flying alongside escort aircraft and even sent up some planes as targets for gunnery training.

The B17 Flying Fortress bombers started arriving in Huntingdonshire during the autumn of 1942. By the end of October, thirty-four Flying Fortresses had

USAAF personnel outside the control tower at Alconbury. (County Record Office Huntingdon: 4336/2 part)

The memorial to the 303rd Bombardment Group, 'Hell's Angels', which stands today at RAF Molesworth. (The authors)

arrived at Molesworth and the airfield itself was given the name Station 107 of the USAAF. On 27 January 1943 USAAF bombers from Huntingdonshire took part in one of the most important missions of the war, when 'Germany, for the first time, was bombed with American bombs from American aeroplanes, with American crews'. (Lt-Col.Harry D. Gobrecht)

The Americans themselves found England hard to get used to. The 91st Bombardment Group was based at Kimbolton, but the servicemen were not impressed with what they found when they arrived there: only some cold Nissen huts in the middle of a muddy field. At Glatton, most of the ground crews lived in tents. Some officers were luckier, as the USAAF took over some of Huntingdonshire's more attractive residences, including Brampton Grange and Alconbury House, said to have been frequented by Clark Gable and James Stewart.

The highest medal awarded to members of US armed forces is the Congressional Medal of Honour. The first one to be awarded to an airman of the US 8th Air Force was made posthumously to 1st Lt Jack Mathis, based at Molesworth. His B17 was hit by flak over the submarine yards at Vegesack on 18 March 1943. Despite terrible injuries he released the bombs, before dying at his station. There is a Mathis Airport in Texas, named in his honour.

By 1943 the skies over Huntingdonshire were filled with Lancaster bombers and Flying Fortresses. Kimbolton was the home of the most successful of all the 8th Air Force's heavy bomber groups, namely the 379th, which flew 330 missions. There were so many bombers that new airfields were constructed to take them all. The USAAF built themselves a new airfield at Glatton, for instance, based on a 1920s private airstrip. B17 Flying Fortresses of the 457th Bomb Group, known as 'the Fireball Outfit', first arrived there in January 1944. Today it is Peterborough Airport and a memorial to the 457th stands in Conington churchyard.

FAMOUS NAMES

The presence of the US military attracted some famous names to Huntingdonshire. In July 1943, actor Bob Hope and singer Frances Langford put on a show for the American airmen at Brampton and Molesworth. Capt. Clark Gable flew as a photographer on a 303rd Bombardment Group bomber on a mission out of Molesworth in May 1943 and was at a local hotel in July that year. Singer Bing Crosby visited Huntingdonshire on 21 September 1944. In August 1943, Adolphe Menjou, a former star of silent movies and an Oscar nominee, visited Huntingdonshire to entertain the US troops. Young journalist Walter Cronkite was a press reporter in Huntingdonshire, based with the 303rd Bombardment Group at Molesworth. Cronkite later became anchorman for CBS Evening News in America.

There was one unusual consequence of the American stay in Huntingdonshire. The first B17 bomber in the 303rd Bombardment Group to get through twenty-five missions in one piece was *Hell's Angel*, based at Molesworth and so Hell's Angels was adopted as the informal name of the entire group. When the group's personnel left Huntingdonshire and returned to California after the end of the war they liked the name 'Hell's Angels' so much that they kept it for the new groups of motorbike riders which they were forming.

Perhaps the most surprising famous name to pass through Huntingdonshire is that of Goering. 1st-Lt W.G.Goering was the nephew of Luftwaffe *Reichsmarshall* Herman Goering and he flew B17 bombers for the 303rd Bombardment Group, based at Molesworth. On 15 February 1945, 1st-Lt. Goering was taking off to bomb Dresden when his B17 lost control and hit the ground by Molesworth's runway. He and his crew managed to get out before the fully bombed-up aircraft exploded. His uncle, of course, was less fortunate, later being one of the Nazi defendants at the Nuremberg Trials, committing suicide before he could be executed.

CHAPTER 10

'Save until it Hurts': War Savings and Salvage

As the war progressed, the need for salvage became acute. When Scandinavia was occupied by the Germans, Britain lost its entire wood-pulp supply. The fall of Malaysia meant that 90 per cent of the world's rubber supply was in enemy hands. In Hartford, schoolchildren collected paper, rags, bones, rubber, tins and scrap metal once a week. This was described as a model scheme as it saved time and valuable petrol for the official collector.

PAPER

Boy scouts began to collect waste paper in early 1940. Collections were also made by Girl Guides, the WVS and local schools. In January 1942, the Waste Paper Recovery Association launched a national waste paper collection contest, with a prize of £1,000 for those collecting the most paper per head of population. The prize money was donated on the condition that the winning areas would give it to charity. There was extensive publicity for the contest in Huntingdonshire, which resulted in 139 tons being collected across the whole county – 22lb per head. St Ives performed best, collecting over 31 tons (the usual figure was just 1 ton). St Ives won £100 in the national competition, which caused resentment amongst some people from other towns, who claimed that most of the waste had come from Enderby's Paper Mill.

In November 1943, a paper-shredding machine was installed at the B.C. & H. showrooms in George Street, Huntingdon, so that confidential documents could be salvaged. 3½cw of paper was saved in this one initiative. The paper was shredded, sold and the profits went to the Red Cross.

METAL

July 1940 saw 'aluminium week' in Huntingdonshire. Intense efforts were made by the WVS, spurred on by the knowledge that one ton of aluminium could make a

Right: Miss D.M. Fence of Fenstanton collecting salvage, May 1941. (*Hunts Post*)

Below: The Sebastopol Cannon, next to the County Hospital in George Street, was a trophy from the Crimean War. It was removed for salvage, 1942. (County Record Office Huntingdon: PH48/83)

Spitfire. Everything was collected, including pots, pans, cooking utensils, aspirin bottle tops, vacuum cleaners and kettles. Collectors were particularly jubilant about the gift of a water bottle bought in Munich. In Fenstanton, a capacious old pram was lent by Mrs Papworth from the High Street to make the collection easier. Mr Winfield was making house-to-house collections three days a week in Huntingdon and could cover the whole borough in three weeks. Mr Henry Middleton was collecting salvage in Buckden with his horse and cart, despite the fact he was over eighty. Even the Sebastopol Cannon by the County Hospital was removed and broken up for scrap.

The quest for metal meant that iron railings became a target for salvage. These were removed, area by area. Some, such as those at The Chestnuts in Somersham and The Walnut Trees in Bluntisham, were spared due their artistic or historic interest. Iron railings could be exempt on three grounds – for genuine public safety, for preventing livestock from straying or because the railings had historic interest or artistic merit. Inskip Ladds took the third exemption very seriously and personally drew pictures of many railings and gates in Huntingdonshire to justify their retention, drawings which still survive today. Fifty-six tons of railings were collected in St Ives in just sixteen days, but even so, many people did not want to give up their railings. Councillor Stiles commented:

> When we think of the sacrifices the Russians and the Poles have made – their homes destroyed, their wives, sisters and daughters raped – I am surprised that some of the people of this town, in their smugness, can raise the question of making a little sacrifice by giving up a few iron railings.

A. Allion of St Ives wrote in a letter to the *Hunts Post* that:

> I should like to commiserate with the unfortunate few in St Ives who have been deprived of the privilege of helping their country in its hour of need by being allowed to retain their (in most cases) quite unnecessary gates or railings. I hope they are feeling comfortable in their natural surroundings – behind bars.

THE BOOK DRIVES

In August 1942 there was a two-week salvage drive, in which old books were the main target, although anything was accepted. The aim of the campaign was to bring home the importance of salvage, to improve collection and to inform as to what was wanted. Paper was needed for shell cases, gun fuses and bomb containers; rags for uniforms, blankets and overcoats; linen for making maps and charts. Bones were used for making nitro-glycerine for high explosives, glycerine for medical use, lubricating grease for tanks, glue for camouflage paint and aircraft construction and for fertiliser. Metal was needed for fighter planes,

A drawing made by arshitect Inskip Ladds of the iron gates at Diddington Hall, as evidence of their architectural and historical worth. (County Record Office, Huntingdon)

bombers, torpedoes, mines, machine-gun barrels, tanks, bayonets and helmets. Rubber was recycled into tyres, hot-water bottles, dinghies and 'Mae Wests', gymshoes for commandos and gas masks. Sportsmen were urged to collect and return all fired cartridge cases, so the brass could be salvaged.

During the fortnight, loudspeaker cars broadcast appeals for salvage, special films were shown and shops put up window displays of items made from salvage. Vicars were asked to sort through old hymn books. Many places aimed to lay out a mile of books. In Ramsey the trail started at Palmers Corner and continued along Great Whyte. In St Ives, the mile of books ran from Barclay's Bank along The Waits. In Huntingdon a bookstall was very popular – those who brought along three or four books could take away one in exchange. In total around 1,350 were collected. All the books were checked by a librarian, Mr Charles Newman, who saved several items of value and interest from destruction.

Later in the war, a second book drive was held, this time to send books to men and women of the forces serving abroad after the invasion. Anything rare or valuable was sorted out to help restock libraries destroyed in the Blitz. Schoolchildren were set the task of collecting the books and would be awarded a military rank, according to the number they returned with. The scheme was very successful and the Huntingdon Book Recovery Army was said to be the only one in which field marshalls and generals outnumbered the privates. The final book drive of the period came at the end of the war when the county was set a target of 124,000

Children collecting books for the Book Drive, July 1944. (*Hunts Post*)

books and magazines to send to service men and women who now had considerably more time on their hands! It is a wonder that there were any books left, but amazingly the target was smashed within weeks.

SALVAGE SUCCESS

Salvage drives meant the usual round of dances and whist drives, the price of admission being a piece of salvage. In Huntingdon, over 2,000 people visited a salvage exhibition. In one such drive, Godmanchester achieved the highest amount of income from salvage per head of population in the whole of England, with £57 per 1,000 people. The next highest was Canterbury with £39 4s per 1,000. However, the real key was to encourage sustained endeavour.

In February 1943, T.H. Longstaff, honorary district advisor for salvage, estimated that local salvage efforts had saved 200 return journeys across the Atlantic. A WVS county clothing store was opened at 24 High Street, Huntingdon, which was a building loaned to the WVS by the RAF. There were five sub-depots, in Fletton, Ramsey, St Ives, St Neots and Eynesbury. Second-hand clothes were sold and gifts from the USA and the Dominions were distributed.

Shortages in other areas led to ingenious methods of salvage. In what became known as the 'Woodwalton mines' a group of schoolchildren, working under the direction of a Mrs Hall, made briquettes out of coal dust and cement and sold them to householders in lieu of coal. They made a profit of £10 in under a year.

SPONTANEOUS FUNDRAISING

Huge efforts were put into raising funds for different projects. The Earl and Countess of Sandwich were often at the forefront of these efforts and Hinchingbrooke House was more often than not the venue for fêtes and such like. Many different means of raising money were tried. At the fête held in July 1940, £6 was raised by the sale of a 1928 magnum of champagne from the cellars of Hinchingbrooke and a bowls contest raised £11. A picture of Hitler which appeared among the portraits of the Earl of Sandwich's ancestors in the art gallery, entitled *First Earl of Berchtesgaden*, was used for target practice. Lord Sandwich had his own 'comforts fund' which provided anti-aircraft posts with easy chairs, settees and tables and also provided wool for knitting items for the troops.

The Spitfire Fund was a spontaneous national reaction to the heroics of the airmen defending Britain in August 1940. In a letter, the Mayor of Godmanchester

The Duchess of Gloucester and Lord Sandwich at Huntingdon's Red Cross fête, August 1941. (*Hunts Post*)

explained that, 'the magnificent exploits of the Royal Air Force, besides commanding the admiration of all classes of the community, have aroused a national
desire to express that admiration in tangible form by the provision of Spitfires for
the continuance of their heroic efforts.' Lord Sandwich urged people to concentrate their efforts on behalf of the Red Cross, but the Spitfire Fund went ahead
anyway in Godmanchester and St Ives. The target was £5,000 which would buy
one Spitfire. The following week, Huntingdon, St Neots and Ramsey had joined
in. Mr R.G. Parker of St Ives promised 100 guineas if twelve other individuals or firms would match it. He said 'as a soldier who served in the last war, I
know that... many, both in and out of the services would rather have fighters and
bombers than comforts etc, should there be insufficient funds for both'.

Employees at Chivers and the Hosiery Mills planned to set up their own fund
and members of Huntingdon Golf Club had already raised £20. St Neots was the
first town to raise £1,000. Sir William Prescott, of the Chestnuts, Godmanchester,
was coordinating the county fund. In a magnificent gesture, Mr J.A. Fielden of
Holme sent a cheque for £50,000 to the Chancellor of the Exchequer, enough
for ten Spitfires. He followed this up with two more contributions of £10,000
in 1940 and in 1941. One of the Spitfires purchased by Mr Fielden was named
Holmewood I and was later reported to have shot down four Luftwaffe planes. One
of its pilots was a pilot officer from Trinidad.

Soon every village was holding house-to-house collections and a range of social
events, in addition to the profusion of events to raise money for comforts for the
troops. Even troops serving overseas sent in contributions: seven Somersham men
for example sent 10s. Two boys, Edward and David Ground of Great Staughton,
raised £1 by giving 500 rides on their pony 'Tommy', mainly to evacuees. Not
everyone was fully behind the war effort though: £2 15s 6d was stolen from
the Spitfire Fund collection at the Comrades Club in Godmanchester. The thief,
however, when on bail in London, was so shocked by the air-raid damage that he
repaid £1.

The fund was finally closed in December 1940, having raised £6,336 16s 1d.
Soon it was dubbed 'the fund that would not die', as money kept coming in. By
February 1941, £6,405 had been raised.

THE NATIONAL FUNDRAISING DRIVES

The success of the Spitfire Fund led to a series of special fundraising initiatives.
The first was 'War Weapons Week' in 1941. Unlike the Spitfire Fund, War Weapons
Week was a savings drive whereby money was invested in savings stamps rather
than donated outright. The people of Huntingdonshire were asked to 'save till
it hurts' and the target was set at £200,000. Savings groups were being set up
everywhere. There were twenty-seven in Huntingdon and Godmanchester and

PROTECTORS—OLD STYLE AND NEW

St Ives Home Guard parading
at the opening of War Weapons
Week, March 1941. (*Hunts Post*)

The plaque commemorating
HMS *Ramsey*, displayed today at
St Ives Town Hall. (The authors)

twenty in Ramsey. The WVS group in Huntingdon had over 300 members and they planned to visit every house in Huntingdon to urge people to buy savings stamps. Mr Fielden again set the ball rolling, with £40,000 (this was a gift rather than a loan). Several insurance companies and banks chipped in with £1,000 each. Events and exhibitions were held across the county during March, including a touring display featuring a Messerschmitt aircraft. Half the total target had been subscribed before the week even began and the final total was more than treble the £200,000 hoped for (£676,933), more than £12 per head of population. Sixty-two new savings groups were also formed during War Weapons Week.

March 1942 saw 'Warship Week', which had massive publicity in the *Hunts Post*. Much was made of the naval links of the county through Samuel Pepys and the Sandwich family, which had close links to the Admiralty. An added incentive was the fact that money raised would go to HMS *Ramsey*. Huntingdonshire was one of only a few counties to have a warship named after one of its towns. HMS *Ramsey* was one of fifty ships handed over by the USA in 1940 and it had been constantly involved in the Battle of the Atlantic, visiting Canada, Iceland and northern Russia.

The woodwork department of Huntingdon Grammar School made a 30ft-high 'indicator' to show progress towards the target of £700,000. The eighty-one-year-old squire of Holme, Mr Fielden, again started things off well by investing £20,000. The London Brick Co. invested £25,000 and Pearl Assurance Co. Ltd £5,000. Scotneys Sawmills of St Ives aimed to raise £1,000 to provide the sickbay on HMS *Ramsey*. In fact they achieved savings of over £2,000. Most of the money was raised by a series of events: parades, exhibitions, demonstrations, dances, whist drives, plays and concerts. There was a dominoes tournament in Sawtry, a searchlight demonstration in the Great Whyte in Ramsey and exhibitions featuring photographs of local men serving in the Navy. A gigantic darts tournament was organised in Huntingdon. 118 teams took part and there were eleven dartboards on the go during the early rounds. The 'Horseshoes' at Offord defeated the 'Three Tuns' of Huntingdon in the final. King Peter of Yugoslavia took part in another darts match in Great Gransden. A total of £609,854 was raised – £10 17s per head, less than the target of £12 per head, but a splendid effort nevertheless.

Schemes such as this were vital to the war effort because in 1942 the war was costing £150 a second, day and night. The gap between income and expenditure could only be met by borrowing, which is by people lending money to the government through war savings schemes. War savings went on continuously. In the Huntingdon and Godmanchester area, almost a third of the population belonged to a savings group. There were sixty-nine such groups, including nineteen places of employment, twenty-nine schools, seven street groups and fourteen social institutions. Initiatives, such as Warship Week, gave a further incentive for people to redouble their efforts. Warship Week was followed later in 1942 by a 'Tanks for

"Wings for Victory"

HUNTINGDON AND DISTRICT
Have gladly accepted the Challenge issued by
ST. IVES AND DISTRICT

: **THERE IS NO NEED TO ASK THE** :
QUESTION AS TO WHO SHALL
: **WEAR THE NEW HAT** :

THE MAYOR OF HUNTINGDON HAS ALREADY
DISPOSED OF HIS OLD ONES AND WILL BE
READY FOR THE "CORONATION" ON
APRIL 10th.

BUT, HUNTINGDON, HE RELIES ON YOU

SAVE to LEND — LEND for LIBERTY

"Wings for Victory" Week
April 3rd to 10th

This space has been kindly presented to the "WINGS FOR
VICTORY" Committee by MURKETT BROS., Motor Engineers,
Huntingdon.

A 'Wings for Victory' advert from the *Hunts Post* of March 1943, featuring
the Huntingdon *v* St Ives hat challenge. (*Hunts Post*)

St Ives, Huntingdon and Brampton planned the concept of the 'beautiful bomb'. An empty bomb casing was covered with war savings stamps. It was then filled with explosives by the RAF and dropped over Germany, April 1943. (*Hunts Post*)

Attack' scheme. By increasing savings by 40 per cent, Godmanchester qualified to have its name on a tank. Ramsey saved £17,917 which meant that two Churchill tanks were allocated to the town.

WINGS FOR VICTORY

The drive in 1943 was named 'Wings for Victory' and was launched in Huntingdon by King Peter of Yugoslavia, the nineteen-year-old great-grandson of Queen Victoria. His mother, Queen Marie launched the campaign in St Neots. Each district set its own targets: St Ives aimed to invest £50,000, enough for ten Spitfires, while Huntingdon aimed for £120,000 for three Lancaster bombers. Within the districts, small areas also set their own goals. Houghton Road in St Ives wanted to raise £17 10s for five pairs of flying boots and Slepe Hall £70 for two parachutes.

As usual, the organisers and local officials came up with new ideas to spice up the appeal. The Mayor of St Ives challenged the Mayor of Huntingdon to see which town could raise the most. The loser would buy the other a new hat. In the end, both St Ives and Huntingdon smashed their targets, but St Ives won the challenge. St Ives's Mayor magnanimously suggested that the cost of his new hat should be given to the Red Cross. Huntingdon and St Ives were not the only success stories – Diddington raised £1,420 – over £60 per head of population.

The drive in 1944 was 'Salute the Soldier' week. This time each district had a distinct week between April and October rather than all sharing the same week. There was again a challenge between the mayors of St Ives and Huntingdon boroughs as to which community could raise the most per head. This time the loser would provide a live pig to the winner. The Mayor of Godmanchester joined in the fun and issued a similar challenge to his counterpart in Huntingdon, prompting Councillor Beardmore (Huntingdon's Mayor) to appeal to the townsfolk, 'I hope that if you think anything of your Mayor you will not let me scour the county for a brace of live pigs.'

Huntingdon's 'Salute the Soldier' week saw a huge parade of over 1,000 military personnel from the Army, RAF and Home Guard. The Market Square was decorated with bunting and the flags of the United Kingdom, US, Russia and China were flying. Even the tiny village of Colne held five events during their 'Salute the Soldier' week. All savings records were broken: Huntingdon smashed its target of £50,000 by almost £35,000. Even this was not enough to save Councillor Beardmore's bacon though. Although Huntingdon's £7 15s per head beat Godmanchester's £4 14s and won the pig, Salute the Soldier Week in St Ives was yet to take place. With impeccable timing, St Ives held their savings week just as the long-awaited invasion took place and thus ran away with the bet raising a huge £11 per head. The pigs were purchased at St Ives Market on 10 July and then auctioned again, several times, including once to the Mayor of St Ives, who paid £9 10s. The pigs finally raised £70 for the Red Cross Agriculture Fund before finally being sold to a Mr J.H. Billings for £10 12s.

FUNDING THE RED CROSS

Although these special fundraising and savings schemes received huge publicity, the effort to raise money continued unceasingly, week after week. People were asked to dig deep for every possible cause. The Red Cross 'Penny a Week Fund' was founded in November 1939 and operated in most villages. Penny a week collectors going from door to door between March 1943 and February 1944 collected £6,228 across Huntingdonshire. Events such as the annual fête at Hinchingbrooke and the weekly whist drive in the band room at Ramsey were held to raise money. The Hinchingbrooke fête was always popular and was always attended by the Duchess of Gloucester. In 1941 between 5–6,000 people attended. 1,500 of them paid 6d each to see the famous St Neots Quads, dressed in sailors' outfits, 'at home' in the little playhouse in the grounds. In 1941 the Red Cross 'Sports Fund' was launched. The idea was that money would be raised by

A 'Salute the Soldier' advert from the *Hunts Post*, April 1944, showing the individual targets set by Huntingdonshire's towns.

ANN CURTSEYS TO THE DUCHESS

Ann Miles, one of the St Neots Quads, curtseys to the Duchess of Gloucester at Hinchingbrooke's Red Cross fête, August 1941. (*Hunts Post*)

sports organisations. There were bowls, darts, football, hockey and tennis tournaments. Mrs Elphick agreed to host outdoor whist drives in her garden. Over £7,000 was raised by this means.

From 1942, the Red Cross were asking that more money be found due to the increased costs of providing parcels for prisoners of war. The work of the Red Cross was estimated to cost £9 a minute in 1942, so continuous fundraising was essential. The cost of sending weekly parcels of food to Huntingdonshire POWs in Germany and Italy was £2,860 a year. In November 1942, POW week raised over £11,000 in Huntingdonshire, the equivalent of 5s per head. This was, of course in addition to the amounts already invested in war savings by Huntingdonshire's population. The commitment to helping out those in enemy hands never faltered – during POW week in 1944 Ramsey Heights raised over £1,000, over £1 per head of population. Returning POWs like Pte Joe Bailey of St Ives paid heartfelt thanks to the Red Cross for their efforts. In many cases, they said, the Red Cross parcels had kept them alive. He had been working a twelve-hour day, seven days

Federal Steam Navigation Company's "M.V. Huntingdon" 11284 tons

The SS *Huntingdon*, sunk by the German Kriegsmarine, 1942. (County Record Office Huntingdon: MD5/17/4)

a week in a German mine on very meagre rations and had depended on the parcels.

GIVING AID ABROAD

After the German invasion of Russia in June 1941 Mrs Churchill's 'Aid to Russia' Fund was another popular cause. The first Anglo-Soviet weekend was held in November 1941. The aim was to foster understanding between the two nations as well as to raise money. As Alderman W.E. Driver put it, 'we must never forget that but for an unexpected accident of war it might have been our land that was shattered by the invader'. The Anglo-Soviet Friendship Committee organised lectures and exhibitions about all things Russian, language classes, films and discussion groups. Between October and December 1941, income from the Red Cross 'penny a week' fund was used for aid to Russia. In 1942, the committee was fundraising for a mobile X-ray unit for use in Russia. 'Red Army Day' was officially celebrated on 25 February 1943, its twenty-fifth anniversary. Children in schools learnt about Russia – there was even a children's essay competition on Russia. As the war in the east progressed, an 'Aid to China' fund was set up too.

As well as supporting national causes, local communities were asked to raise money for local men serving with the forces. This money was generally sent off via the British Legion. Amounts varied from place to place. At Christmas 1942, for example, the 158 men from Brampton, Spaldwick, Ellington and Easton serving in the forces received a postal order for 7s 6d; those from Alconbury received 30s and the twenty-two men and four women from Colne were sent a princely £4 10s each. Colne also gave 10s to each evacuee and sent a parcel to its one POW. St Neots and District British Legion sent 260,000 cigarettes to local men serving overseas and POWs in 1943.

Nor were other causes forgotten, 'Air Raid Distress Fund', 'Woollen Fund', 'Comforts for the Troops' and 'Comforts for Evacuees' all still received donations. The 'Cancer Research Fund' was aided by a dance held at the Brampton Institute, with a prize draw for cigarettes! Huntingdonshire's Air Raid Distress Fund effort of over £900 merited a special mention at the meeting of the Executive Committee at St James' Palace in 1941.

Every conceivable way of raising money was employed. The presence of Charlie Garner, BBC darts commentator, in the area (he became proprietor of the Oliver Cromwell pub in St Ives) was responsible for a darts boom in the county. One tournament to raise money for Mrs Churchill's Aid to Russia Fund had 163 teams of four taking part, with another 146 playing as pairs. Fundraising dances and whist drives were held several times a week in the towns and many villages. Concerts, fêtes and sales were a regular occurrence. Auctions were another popular way of making money. Usually the same things would be sold again and again – during POW week in Ramsey in 1942, a single box of matches raised £3 7s 6d. Often lemons or bananas, which had been sent from overseas, were auctioned or raffled to raise money.

In September, 'Vicky', the Victory V calf, toured the county, visiting St Ives and St Neots. This calf raised money for the Red Cross Agricultural Fund by visiting local markets. She had two baskets on her shoulders and people simply put money in them – over £124 was raised at St Ives market in this way. Nationally, the calf had raised over £13,000.

As well as helping out the military, the people of Huntingdon were asked to 'adopt' a merchant ship, the SS *Huntingdon*. Locals would provide the crew with woollen hats, socks and pullovers, cigarettes and chocolate, etc. Unfortunately, soon after it was adopted by the county, the SS *Huntingdon* was attacked by a submarine and sunk. The county agreed to sponsor the SS *Empire Progress* instead.

'Sheer Physical Exhaustion': The Final Years

By Christmas 1943, there was real hope that the coming year would see the end of the war. The New Year of 1944 was seen in by a peal of bells, the first for many years. Planning for post-war Huntingdonshire began in earnest. Post-war housing, electoral reform and other issues were widely discussed. Towns and villages began 'welcome home' funds and began collections for 'Victory Halls' to be built in honour of those fighting in the war.

Just because the tide of war had turned permanently against Germany, Huntingdonshire could still not let its defences slip. A real danger still existed from 1944 onwards in the form of German V-weapons, aimed at London but occasionally crashing off-course. Upwood parish church had its windows smashed by a V1 explosion on 25 January 1944. A further 190 properties, including 183 domestic houses, were damaged in Somersham on 18 March 1945, when a V1 exploded near the church. A pair of V1s flew also over the Offords one day: one crashed into empty fields just past Offord while the other carried on towards Kimbolton. I.B. Hunter saw one of these fly past, 'One evening I stood and looked out of the back bedroom window and a Doodle Bug passed only 50ft away. It was long and sleek and silver, gushing out flames. Within a second it cut out. I understand that the Doodle Bug fell in a field near Offord.'

Huntingdonshire's bombers did try to fight back against the V-weapons. On 18 July 1944, B17 Flying Fortresses from Molesworth attacked Peenemunde, on the north German coast, where Werner Von Braun and other German scientists were developing the V2 rockets.

At the same time, Allied forces were gearing up for the invasion of German-occupied Europe. Training courses were run for the WVS volunteers in March 1944, on how to 'make do and mend' – preparing for the forthcoming invasion and the expected backlash from the Germans. Knitting was still being done in huge quantities, but it was not the troops who needed the knitters this time: instead the appeals were made to 'clothe the people of liberated Europe.'

By April 1944, it was almost time for the Czech soldiers to leave. Their unit presented an illuminated crest hand-painted on silk to Huntingdon Borough

A German V1 'Doodlebug' on its launch ramp, at the Imperial War Museum Duxford. (The authors)

Council in appreciation of the happy time they had spent in the town. They also presented a signed copy of *The Spirit of Bohemia* to the chairman of the Services Club in Huntingdon. Even after they had left, messages were received by their friends in Huntingdon:

> We have not yet found the contact with the new people that we had at your lovely old town. It hurt to go away from there and every one of our boys was sorry as they felt at home there and were treated like adopted sons and not as strangers. Please express our thanks to all the people there and we hope many of our friends will pay us a visit in our liberated Czechoslovakia.

In April 1944, the county began to stockpile blood for use in the forthcoming invasion. When it finally came, in June, maps of France appeared in Huntingdonshire stationers' shops. People studied them intensely and stood about in groups discussing the latest radio bulletins. Services were held in local churches. Scotney's workforce listened to the radio at work and was addressed by Revd Bitten.

Able Seaman Ray Nicholls, aged twenty, of Westwood Road in St Ives was one of the first men taking part in the Normandy invasion, actively trying to detonate mines with mortar and machine-gun fire. It was not long before news of the first casualties of the invasion was reported in the *Hunts Post*. Sgt Anthony English from Perry and Signaller Alexander Simpson from Broughton were both killed in the first few days.

Hunts HOME GUARD, 2nd Batt.

urgently requires gift or loan of SPORTS GEAR
to enable them to form FOOTBALL AND CRICKET TEAMS.

Items chiefly needed are —

FOOTBALLS	CRICKET BATS
BOOTS	STUMPS
JERSEYS & SHORTS	BALLS
STOCKINGS	PADS AND GLOVES

Also **BAND INSTRUMENTS AND MUSIC**

Phone St. Ives 3296, or write:—
HEADQUARTERS, 20, Broadway, St. Ives.

By courtesy of Mr. A. Steadman, Jeweller, Huntingdon.

This advert in the *Hunts Post* for sports equipment indicates how much easier life was becoming for Huntingdonshire's Home Guard in 1944.

Farewell to the Home Guard, 1944. (*Hunts Post*)

As the fighting intensified in France, the fear of invasion receded at home. Concrete roadblocks, erected to slow down an invading force, began to be removed. In September 1944 barbed wire was being removed from all over St Ives. Street lights began to come on again. Confidence was high – by October

1944, Brampton already had its victory day service planned. The *Hunts Post* featured tales of local soldiers' exploits in France. One Warboys man, whose father had been killed in France in 1918, was able to visit his grave. Another POW, Gunner Edward Deighton from Brampton, was liberated by a group of men which included his brother Ernie.

After the Normandy landings, many members of the Huntingdonshire Home Guard had left for coastal and other operational duties to relieve regular troops. As the invasion progressed, the Home Guard was able to take things more easily and, towards the end of 1944, it began to wind down. Parades were held across the county and weapons were handed in. Platoon photographs were taken. The final parade of the Home Guard took place on 7 December 1944. In Huntingdon 700 men of the 2nd Battalion mustered on Mill Common and marched via St Mary's Street, along the High Street to Market Hill. They continued up Ambury Road to the old grammar school, where they were addressed by Col. Wilson. He took the salute and commented: 'you have helped to stave off the invasion: you have helped to turn defeat into the coming victory: you have done your duty honourably and well.' Lt-Col. Duberly took the salute of the 3rd (South) Hunts Battalion in St Neots Market Square on 3 December 1944. The Home Guard was not officially disbanded, however, until the war was over. Home Guard members had to return their guns and ammunition, but they were allowed to keep their uniforms and boots.

In 1945, the WVS in Huntingdonshire began collecting household items for those whose homes had been bombed. This was known as the 'Good Neighbour Gift Scheme.' Huntingdon 'adopted' the town of Billericay in Essex. Goods were collected at a depot in the Norman Hall (today's Cromwell Museum) and sent in van loads to the adopted town. Housewives in Billericay were reported to view the gifts as 'an absolute godsend', particularly the kitchen equipment, china and linens.

CELEBRATING VICTORY

In 1945, people's thoughts began to turn to the coming victory. Prisoners of War were being liberated from camps in Germany and were returning home to families in Huntingdonshire. Cpl Frederick Wright of the Royal Corps of Signals arrived home at 58 Cowper Road in August 1944 as the first liberated prisoner of war to return to Huntingdon. Cpl Wright had a sister in the ATS and a brother in the army. Victor Darnell, son of Mrs Arnold of 42 Cowper Road, had also been a prisoner for five years, being released in March 1945. Another Cowper Road resident, Mrs Verral of number 35, learned that her son, Pte Flisher, had been liberated by the American 9th Army in May. He had been captured at Oudenarde in May 1940, set to work on a farm, then transferred to Marionberg and elsewhere.

Some of the 17.5 tons of 'Good Neighbour Gifts' sent to Billericay in Essex, April 1945. (*Hunts Post*)

Typical of many returning POWs he thanked the Red Cross – 'from the bottom of my heart' – for the parcels which had kept them going.

Local communities began to raise funds – nothing new there – but this time the funds were to celebrate the coming victory. Brampton and Somersham were just two communities who planned to build village halls as a peace memorial. In Huntingdon, a committee was formed to decide how best to celebrate victory. The chairman, Alderman Clayton, expressed its aims, 'We are not out for a Mafeking night but have tried to draw up a modest programme which will meet the case but which will not hurt the feelings of those who have lost loved ones in the war.'

When the German surrender was announced on 8 May churches were packed for thanksgiving services, flags fluttered everywhere, bells were rung and bonfires lit. Girls wore red, white and blue ribbons in their hair. Both cinemas in Huntingdon opened to show the newsreels. Shops, factories and most offices were closed for two days and public houses were given a special VE day extension until 11.30 p.m., although most had run out of beer long before then.

Individual communities expressed their joy in different ways. Ingram Street in Huntingdon set up a large wooden 'V' sign decorated with red, white and blue electric bulbs. In the same town, residents of St Germain Street hung lines of red, white and blue washing across the street. In Fenstanton, boys from the ATC rode around on bicycles with lighted torches.

The VE Day parade by Huntingdonshire's WAAFs. (Jean Matthews)

Churchill's speech to the nation was relayed to a large crowd on Huntingdon's Market Hill during Tuesday afternoon. At 8.50 p.m. the Mayor came out on the Town Hall balcony to address the throng before the King's speech at 9.00 p.m. was relayed to the crowd.

Large numbers of people danced in the centres of all the market towns until the early hours. In St Ives, a large crowd, which included American and Polish officers, danced in a giant conga around a huge bonfire. By the morning, Oliver Cromwell's statue had acquired a dustbin lid on its head. In the Ramsey area, a chair was found affixed to the steeple of a church. In Huntingdon, a WAAF climbed on the war memorial and placed a cigarette between the soldier's lips, offending many of the more sober residents. As the celebrations continued, the fire service was kept busy putting out fires, including numerous blazing haystacks. Street parties, fancy-dress parades and victory sports events were held all across the county.

Amongst all the celebrations, years of thrift were not forgotten. The WVS went round collecting the redundant blackout material. It was to be used to make black pinafores for French schoolchildren.

Once the celebrations had died down, people began to ponder on a suitable memorial for those who had given their lives. A lengthy public meeting was held in Huntingdon, but no decision had been reached after two and a half hours of discussion. The overall feeling was for a hall or community centre, but a proposal to acquire the American Red Cross hostel in Hodges Close was defeated. In the end a committee was formed to investigate the matter. A second public meeting, in July 1945, agreed that there should be a memorial hall which would seat 600, have a stage and a floor suitable for dancing. Fundraising for the new hall was very disappointing however, in contrast to the success of the wartime collections.

THE RETURNING SOLDIERS

On 23 June Wireman W.T. Hayward RN arrived home in Cowper Road, the first Huntingdonian to be demobilised. He was wearing his 'demob suit', which was described as being dark in colour, with four pockets in the waistcoat, four in the jacket and another three in the trousers, which also had some stylish turn-ups. The quality of the fabric was held to be 'good'. In Holywell-cum-Needingworth, the British Legion organised a village social in October 1945, which raised £10 towards the homecoming fund for servicemen. In the same month, Mervyn Coote gave the St Ives branch of the British Legion its present home in St Ives Broadway.

As Huntingdonshire's own servicemen began to arrive home, those from overseas began to leave England. The US 8th Air Force planned to donate their radios, bicycles and electrical appliances to charitable organisations. The need for secrecy

USAAF airmen at Alconbury. (County Record Office Huntingdon: 4336/2 part)

was over and the USAAF held an open day at Alconbury to commemorate their 38th anniversary. The open day attracted 10,000 visitors. The Americans also held formal parades on their airfields. At Molesworth, trips were organised for all non-combat personnel to fly over ruined German cities, to enable them to see the damage they had helped to cause. The Americans left quite quickly, of course, as they foresaw the need to have as many bombers as possible in the Pacific in readiness for the anticipated invasion of Japan.

As the Americans began to leave, those who had married American servicemen prepared to leave England for good and make a new life in the United States. Special meetings were held for them at the American Red Cross Services Club to prepare the women for life in America. Mrs Attwood, director of the club, warned that 'America was not all that the movies pretended'. The GI brides club in Huntingdon met for lectures about American cooking. They would be able to travel free to join their husbands, but they had to be ready to travel at short notice. Just as Huntingdonshire's women were going to join their American husbands, Huntingdon also prepared to welcome overseas brides here. Mrs Adeline Dunford, whose husband was a Petty Officer in the Fleet Air Arm, was expected from Australia to settle in Wyton.

NUCLEAR SECRETS

From July to December 1945, ten leading German scientists were held quietly at Farm Hall in Godmanchester. They had been taken into American custody in Germany and flown to Tempsford, removed from Germany before the Russians arrived because many believed that they were further advanced in the production of a nuclear bomb than the Americans. Farm Hall had been requisitioned in 1942 by the British secret service and used to train agents before they were flown into occupied territory. British Intelligence secretly recorded the conversations of the scientists whilst they were held at Farm Hall. One of the men, Otto Hahn, had discovered nuclear fission, which made the atomic bomb possible. When the Americans dropped the bomb on Japan he was devastated and reportedly tried to hang himself in the drawing room at Farm Hall.

VICTORY OVER JAPAN

In August, a second round of celebrations began when victory in the East was finally announced. Sirens and whistles began to sound immediately after Mr Attlee's midnight announcement of the Japanese surrender. Bonfires were lit across the county. Ramsey was lit with searchlights and planes from the Pathfinder stations dropped flares. Two days of celebrations began. Churches were packed for

Farm Hall in Godmanchester, where German nuclear scientists were held during the closing months of the war. (The authors)

VJ Day celebrations, August 1945. (Cambridgeshire Libraries: Y. Hun K.45 772)

THE *JEST* MATCH

ONE OF THE BEST EVENTS in the excellent peace celebrations programme at Huntingdon was the comic cricket match between the Borough Council and a Ladies XI. Left: the Mayor (Coun. E. Hodson) gets some of the right spirit for the game, while his Deputy (Coun. L. G. Beardmore) looks on envyingly. Below: the ceremonial arrival of the Council team and (bottom) a group including all taking part in this most amusing effort.

The 'Jest Match' cricket challenge between men and women, August 1945. (*Hunts Post*)

thanksgiving services, buildings were floodlit and peals of bells rang out. There were also fireworks, despite the fact that Councillor Bradshaw had opposed Huntingdon Town Council's plan to spend £5 on fireworks for VJ Day. 'There have been enough fireworks in the last six years in my opinion,' he said. Fireworks in Alconbury Weston set fire to a thatched cottage – the house was destroyed, but no one was hurt. Hundreds of street parties were held across the county. More sports and fancy-dress parades also took place. In Huntingdon, members of the council took on a team of ladies in a cricket match. The councillors were put in to bat by the ladies. The Mayor and his deputy, dressed in full scarlet regalia, were wheeled to the crease in bath chairs. In the end neither side scored many runs, but the ladies won. Godmanchester had a novelty football match between the RAF and the WAAF. The WAAF scored first, making sure the ball crossed the line by kicking the goalkeeper into the net, too.

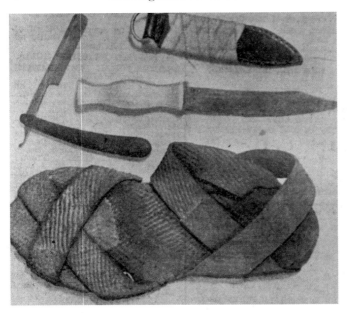

Sandals and a razor brought home by a POW from the Far East, 1945. (*Hunts Post*)

800 children were entertained to tea at the American Red Cross Hostel. Three-thousand people attended a huge bonfire on the Hartford Road playing fields. Figures of Hitler and Hirohito were strung across St Germain Street, while Cowper Road held another street party. Most pubs had, by this time, run out of beer: 'Just after 1 a.m. the dancing stopped. This was earlier than the previous night, yet it was quite clear that this was not through lack of interest, but through sheer physical exhaustion.'

In October, the first POWs from the Far East began to return home, bringing with them tales of the hardships they had suffered. The first to arrive home was L/Cpl John Whall of Alexandra Cottages in Huntingdon. He had been captured in Singapore and made to work on the Malaya-Burma railway. Returning prisoners told how the Red Cross parcels had been stolen and sold by the Japanese soldiers. Locals had supplied bags of sand, disguised as sugar, which were not replaced by their captors and this was held to be the cause of many deaths from starvation. Pte George, from St Ives, told how he and his mates had eaten roast python which they had killed themselves. Others reported eating dog, snake and iguana. Others told how their letters from home had been burnt.

The following year, 8 June 1946 was designated for more victory celebrations. Events were planned across the county. Street teas, fancy-dress parades and the like were planned everywhere. There was dancing in Huntingdon and St Neots Market Squares and the Broadway in St Ives. Among the more unusual events were a parade of decorated vehicles in Somersham, a pillow-fight contest at Holywell-cum-Needingworth, a decorated pram parade in Abbotsley and a

A peace parade on Mill Common, 1946. (County Record Office Huntingdon: PH100A/3)

hunt for hidden treasure at Abbots Ripton. In King's Ripton, the men dressed as women. Unfortunately the weather was awful and many events were washed out or postponed.

THE END

One consequence of the war was a new ghost at the Manor House in Hemingford Grey. Many airmen had attended Lucy Boston's gramophone concerts there over the years, but not all of them had come back from missions over Germany.

> A latecomer was heard coming up the uncarpeted stairs to the music room door, outside which he waited for the record to end. When Elisabeth, as always, rose to open the door, every eye turned to see who was coming, but there was no one there. Thereafter this happened often, and in fact continued for some years after the war whenever I played to friends in the evening. We assumed it was a shadow memory, or haunting wish of a lost airman.

This must have been true for many of the people of Huntingdonshire: families and friends who had lost loved ones, thinking for a fleeting moment that they heard the dead person on the steps, or knocking on the door, or walking across the garden. So the memories lived on, still vivid in the minds of the survivors.

Index

If you are interested in purchasing other books published by Tempus, or in case you have difficulty finding any Tempus books in your local bookshop, you can also place orders directly through our website

www.tempus-publishing.com